New Experiment in Democracy

NEW EXPERIMENT IN DEMOCRACY

THE CHALLENGE FOR AMERICAN CATHOLICISM

DENNIS P. McCANN

Sheed & Ward

For

LESLIE,

BENJAMIN,

and

MATTHEW

Sheed & Ward™ is a service of National Catholic
Reporter Publishing, Inc.

Library of Congress Catalog Card Number: 86-62986

ISBN: 1-55612-000-1

Published by: Sheed & Ward
            115 E. Armour Blvd. P.O. Box 414292
            Kansas City, MO 64141-4292

To order, call: (800) 821-7926

CONTENTS

ACKNOWLEDGEMENTS

This book, more than any of the things I have previously written, is the result of the combined efforts of many persons who have encouraged me and made it possible for me to complete this project. My good friend Dr. John Houck, of the University of Notre Dame, initially suggested that I write a book on the Catholic bishops' pastoral letter on the economy. The Dean of the College of Commerce at De Paul University, and chairman of the University's Committee on Business Ethics, Brother Leo V. Ryan, C.S.V., encouraged me to do so, and provided financial assistance so that I could attend the bishops' hearings held at the University of California at Berkeley in May 1984. My own dean, Dean Richard J. Meister of De Paul's College of Liberal Arts and Sciences, and the College's Committee on Faculty Research and Development, awarded me a Summer Grant during the summer of 1985, so that I could begin the actual writing of the book. Rev. Bruce Vawter, C.M., Chairman of De Paul's Department of Religious Studies, along with Dean Meister, cooperated in arranging my teaching schedule so that I would be free during the Autumn Quarter of 1985 to continue the writing. Justus George Lawler, at that time the editor of Seabury Books for Winston Press, helped me clarify the actual focus of the book: thanks to conversations with him, the book became less a conventional commentary on the pastoral letter on the economy, and more a contextual reading of the pastoral letter process and its historic significance for American Catholicism. I also wish to thank Paul Camenisch, Jack Leahy, and Bob Cooke, all of them my fellow associates at De Paul's Institute for Business Ethics, for their encouragement and support. I have been helped at specific points in this project by conversations with my colleagues and friends, Thomas Duffy, Les Goodchild, Denis Goulet, Ann Graff, David Leege, and Charles Strain. I have benefited from criticisms offered by David J. O'Brien. Finally, and most of all, I am grateful to my friend, Bud Brownsberger, and my wife, Leslie McCann, for having read every word of the first and second drafts of this book. Their editorial criticism has been invaluable. Whatever errors of interpretation and stylistic blunders remain are my own responsibility.

INTRODUCTION

The Catholic Church's New
Experiment in Democracy

Their efforts were arduous and imperfectly realized,
but they launched an experiment in the protection of
civil and political rights that has prospered through
the efforts of those who came after them. We believe
the time has come for a similar experiment in
economic democracy: the creation of an order that
guarantees the minimum conditions for human dignity in the economic sphere for every person.

— Paragraph 89, "Catholic Social Teaching and the
U.S. Economy: The First Draft"

Nothing in the Catholic bishops' pastoral letter on the U.S.
economy has proven more controversial than its call for a "New
American Experiment in Democracy." This proposal has become
the source of anger and consternation among neoconservatives
who fear that the bishops, all their protestations to the contrary
notwithstanding, indeed are closet radicals, even socialists. It
has also inspired hopeful enthusiasm among beleaguered liberals desperately looking for allies in any quarter. Despite the fact
that the objectives of this "New Experiment" are solidly
grounded in the tradition of Catholic social teaching, the controversy surrounding it has been fueled by our lack of clarity concerning the process envisioned for the experiment, its scope, and
its applicability to economic institutions.

1

Greater clarity in understanding the bishops' public agenda is always welcome. But more may be needed here, if their "New American Experiment in Democracy" is to be taken seriously. The pastoral letter on the economy, along with its predecessor on war and peace, are the first fruits of a great awakening now occurring in the American Catholic church, an awakening that will lose its force unless the church transforms itself first, along the lines envisioned in the new experiment. Credibility, in short, requires that the church itself must lead the way, and democratize its own institutional routines as a model for other forms of association in our society. For the church to practice what it preaches, however, it must renew both its practices and its preaching with a vision of American Catholicism that is broader, more daring, and actually more faithful to the historic experience of the church in this country than what so far has appeared in the pastoral letters.

Such a vision is hardly grasped by noting, as the pastoral letter on the economy does, that the church itself is an economic institution whose managerial practices must conform to its stated moral principles. However innovative it may seem for bishops to explicitly recognize the rights of church employees to a "decent remuneration" and collective bargaining, and however sincere may be their solemn assurances of financial accountability, such concessions only scratch the surface of what American Catholicism holds out as the ideal of social justice. Were the bishops to practice what they preach even in this limited way they, no doubt, would create quite a stir. But however impressive the results, a shift in the style of church management is still not quite a "New American Experiment in Democracy."

To practice what it preaches, the church must examine itself in light of Catholic social teaching's currently ruling metaphor of justice as participation. As the pastoral letter on the economy makes clear, justice empowers persons for participation in society and injustice is any personal action, institutional policy, or social structure that discourages participation, or in effect marginalizes persons. The "New American Experiment in Democracy" is a framework for policy reform on a variety of political and economic issues, based on the assumption that justice as participation cannot be achieved so long as democratic processes of self-government are confined to the realm of politics. The bishops' analysis of poverty, for example, concludes that the problem is not inequality of income as such, but the resulting inequality of chances to participate in the processes by which public decisions are made, that actually shape the quality of our common life together. Justice thus means compensating for whatever political and economic forces perpetuate societal patterns of marginalization; it means empowering all persons for civic participation by fostering procedures of effective self-government, not only in politics but also in the economy. The metaphor of justice as participation, in other words, serves as a general guideline for implementing the bishops' moral teaching regarding human dignity and global solidarity.

But however lofty the religious and ethical ideals that resonate in this metaphor, justice as participation will be dismissed as one more ideological hangover from the 1960s so long as the church exempts its own internal governance from the "New American Experiment in Democracy." For a claim to moral seriousness soon becomes implausible in the face of special pleading. If marginalization is a serious threat to human dignity and solidarity, it is no less a threat in the church than it is in society. If, in the name of justice as participation, business corporations are to be prodded into experiments enhancing, among other things, the involvement of workers in management decision-making processes, justice as fairness requires that religious corporations undertake similar experiments. Because of their inevitable tendency to marginalize some members of any given group, hierarchical forms of organization legitimately are to be placed under a certain moral burden of proof. But if in the name of a "New American Experiment in Democracy" this burden is to be placed upon economic as well as political institutions, it should be placed upon religious institutions as well. The church, then, cannot expect to have its social teaching taken seriously, either by ordinary Catholics or by the public at large, if it wavers on this point.

This relatively obvious plea for moral consistency, of course, could not be made had the bishops themselves not provided an opportunity for it. Relying on statements issued by the Synod of Bishops in Rome in 1971, the first draft of the pastoral letter on the economy does give qualified endorsement to the idea that Catholic social teaching also applies to the church as one more "sinful human community." The American Catholic bishops seem to be sincere in their new openness to critical scrutiny. What is lacking, at least in their pastoral letters, is any acknowledgement of either the scope of the internal reform needed for consistency's sake or the uniquely American context in which the plea for it is raised. It is as if the bishops are slowly recovering from a bout of collective amnesia that still clouds their vision of an authentically American Catholicism.

In what follows I hope to dispel the bishops' amnesia and to overcome our own anxieties about the "New American Experiment" by interpreting the pastoral letter on the economy, as well as the recent one on war and peace, in light of the trauma in the history of American Catholicism that accompanied, if not the birth of the church in this country, at least its early childhood. I refer, of course, to the condemnation of the so-called Americanist heresy by Pope Leo XIII at the turn of the century. That preemptive strike against the new form of Catholic religious praxis emerging in this country has tended to make American Catholic church leaders unduly defensive in their approach to American institutions and cultural values. It may help explain why the bishops' pastoral letters themselves appear curiously ungenerous in their estimate of the moral aspirations and achievements of the American people, and strangely ambivalent in their attempt to bring a biblically prophetic perspective to bear on American social and economic practices. Both the ambivalence and the lack of generosity are symptomatic of the psychological damage that may have occurred when the pope condemned "Americanism" as a heresy.

It is as if once upon a time, among the youngest of the Brides of Christ, American Catholicism became frozen in some sort of Elektra complex, unable to mature in her infantile love for her American fatherland because of a repressed conflict with her fiercely protective mother, the church of Rome. Equally protective of her own preferred self-image as a good little girl, this dutiful daughter forgot about the abuse inflicted upon her in early childhood and did her best to please "Holy Mother the Church." Thus her childhood passed in serene obedience, upset occasionally by a mysterious estrangement from the spirit of her American father. But adolescence came, as it inevitably does even to good little girls, when Vatican II disrupted the whole of Christ's rather diverse and far-flung family. After the Council American Catholicism's fragile self-image shattered into a thousand conflicting moods, each as promising of future greatness as it was threatening to the present serenity of the household. The young Bride began to assert herself, but herself she did not yet know. For she had yet to come to terms with her conflicting loves and loving conflicts with her parents.

If this retelling of our story is more than personal whim, it may suggest that the bishops' pastoral letter process stands at the center of this Elektra complex, ambiguously embodying both the church's reawakened awareness of its patriotic responsibilities and its sincere loyalty to the Mother that actually nurtured her. The tension stemming from this unresolved complex is building to a crisis, thanks in part to recent events in the always-precarious history of American Catholicism's relationships with the Vatican. Holy Mother the Church has been reasserting, and possibly even extending, her parental prerogatives lately. She seems particularly jealous of the American bishops' pastoral letter process. The bishops thus find themselves in a difficult position, forced to defend their process in Rome against those distrustful of its democratizing tendencies, yet also eagerly promoting this process because it has given the church a new relationship to American society and culture.

I suggest that the bishops are more likely to resolve this tension creatively if they have the support of a church that has struggled to achieve a moral consensus about its own identity. American Catholics must put aside the evasions of adolescence and face squarely the ambiguity of our past, present, and future. What follows, then, will be an attempt to dispel our collective amnesia. I will outline a theological interpretation of the bishops' pastoral letter process, based on the hunch that what was condemned in Rome as the Americanist heresy is the key to our historic development within the family of Catholic churches. I offer this interpretation in the hope that it will make the pastoral letter process more effective, and thus help the church to live up to the promise of its "New American Experiment in Democracy."

For those who are interested in such matters, let me add a note on methodology. What follows is not an original piece of historical scholarship, nor is it a conventional tract in systematic theology. It is a form of theological reflection that must focus on questions of historical interpretation precisely because it is meant to be practical,that is, it is meant to provide an orientation to strategically important issues currently facing the church. The issue upon which I will concentrate is latent in the church's "New American Experiment in Democracy" and concerns how we are to become accountable to one another: what is the form of governance appropriate to an authentically American Catholic church? The way I will explore that question follows the methodological outline I recently proposed with my colleague Charles R. Strain, *Polity and Praxis: A Program for American Practical Theology*.

Consistent with that proposal, in what follows I focus on Catholic "religious praxis" as providing the basis for theological reflection. By "Catholic religious praxis" I mean more than just the collective experience of Catholic people in this country. By calling it praxis, and not just experience, I am emphasizing the quality of consciousness that accompanies this experience, including timely and provocative theoretical reflections upon it. The point made by this terminology is that doing preceeds knowing. This is central to my argument, for my hope for the "New American Experiment in Democracy" and my sense of the inevitability of the Americanist "heresy" in our thinking about our religious experience in this country, are both based on the assumption that it is the logic of our daily activities, our routine experiences of how we get things done together, that virtually compels us to take our democratic values to church with us. If this assumption is true, then the Americanist "heresy" can never be extirpated, and our democratic aspirations for the church will continue to surface, whether any given group of church leaders finds them congenial or not.

1

THE RETURN OF THE REPRESSED: OWNING UP TO THE AMERICANIST HERESY

This doctrine, which I deliberately call extravagant and absurd, this Americanism as it has been called, has nothing in common with the views, aspirations, doctrine and conduct of Americans.

— James Cardinal Gibbons, Reply to Pope Leo XIII's encyclical letter *Testem benevolentiae*, March 17, 1899

It will be argued that any connection between the condemnation of the Americanist heresy and the recent pastoral letters of the American Catholic bishops ought to remain repressed. Even if a connection were to be discovered, some would consider the mere mention of it inopportune. For to trace the stigma of heresy upon the recent pastoral letters is to risk rekindling the wrath of Rome at a time when Rome seems poised, once more, to extirpate diversity in Catholic religious praxis for the sake of unity within the church. But if the pastoral letters and the controversial response they have generated are to be fully understood, I insist that this risk be taken. The hopes and fears symbolized by the Americanist heresy need to be remembered. Precisely because they have been repressed, they represent a "dangerous memory" for American Catholics.[1] Caught in the amber of a Papal condemnation, these hopes and fears are being liberated by the pastoral letter process today. We must accept them as our own, if that process is to fulfill its historic promise.

Church historians sometimes refer to the Americanist heresy as a "phantom heresy," because in 1899 when the condemnation was issued no one was willing to own up to it. When Cardinal James Gibbons, Archbishop of Baltimore, replied on behalf of the American Catholic hierarchy to Pope Leo XIII, he tried to save the reputation of the Catholic church in this country by denying any connection with this "extravagant and absurd . . . doctrine."[2] Even those bishops most in sympathy with the condemnation merely thanked the Pope for protecting the American church from the "threat" of heresy. While these reactions are understandable, their evasiveness does provoke a question: Was Americanism, then, anything more than a phantom conjured from the fetid night air rising from the Tiber, or were Gibbons and the American hierarchy playing games with Leo XIII?

The Pope's encyclical letter condemning Americanism, *Testem benevolentiae*, ostensibly consists of an unfavorable review of *The Life of Father Hecker*, a biography of the founder of the Paulist Fathers, Isaac Thomas Hecker, written by his ardent disciple, Walter Elliott. This book had come under Vatican surveillance, apparently, because the French translation of it had created quite a stir among Catholics there seeking to work out an accommodation with the new French Republic. The American constitutional principle of separation of church and state, the impressive growth of the American Catholic church under such an arrangement, and Isaac Hecker's own success as an innovative Catholic apologist of international stature had led some French liberals to take Hecker's program of church renewal seriously. Their enthusiasm earned them the label "Americanists" and, not surprisingly, the hostility of powerful conservatives who had yet to reconcile themselves to the demise of the French monarchy. In condemning certain "doctrines" allegedly promoted by Elliott's Hecker, Leo XIII thus was really addressing only the most recent episode in the murky history of

Gallicanism, the name given by generations of Inquisitors to various attempts on the part of Rome's "eldest daughter" to assert an independence from Holy Mother the Church. On this reading, then, the encyclical had nothing to do with America.

Another reading of *Testem benevolentiae* might regard the encyclical as an attempt to nip Catholic modernism in the bud. Like the modernists who were to receive their own condemnation less than a decade later at the hands of Pope Pius X, Elliott's Hecker was faulted for allegedly teaching that "in order the more easily to bring over to Catholic doctrine those who dissent from it, the Church ought to adapt herself somewhat to our advanced civilization, and, relaxing her ancient rigor, show some indulgence to modern popular theories and methods."[3] But this vague charge, so reminiscent in substance, if not style, of Pope Pius IX's *Syllabus of Errors*, implies that, far from being a full-blooded heresy, Americanism is little more than shallow opportunism. Yet the encyclical does not just warn against the watering down of Catholic dogma, it also casts suspicion upon any serious attempt to adapt Catholic religious praxis to the particularities of local circumstances. But this Americanist tendency which later found robust theological justification in the writings of modernists — was it anything more than shameful "indulgence," or did it actually amount to a heresy?

Since even *Testem benevolentiae* concedes that "the rule of life which is laid down for Catholics is not of such a nature as not to admit modifications, according to the diversity of time and place,"[4] the point of the condemnation must lie at a deeper level. What triggered the papal condemnation was the perception that Elliott's Hecker was promoting a "certain liberty" in the church:

> But in the matter of which we are now speaking, Beloved Son, the project involves a greater danger and is more hostile to Catholic doctrine and discipline, inasmuch as the followers of these novelties judge that a certain liberty ought to be introduced into the Church, so that, limiting the exercise and vigilance of

its powers, each one of the faithful may act more
freely in pursuance of his own natural bent and capacity. They affirm, namely, that this is called for in
order to imitate that liberty which, though quite recently introduced, is now the law and the foundation
of almost every civil community.[5]

The Pope's fear of this "certain liberty," because it is itself so un-
seemly, thus provides the clue to yet another reading of the encyclical, one which allows Americanism to be seen in its own
light, apart from the Gallicanisms of the past and a modernism
still in the future. For to place the taboo of heresy upon
Americanism is to proscribe Hecker's vision of the role of the
Catholic laity in the church: Hecker, indeed, did believe that
since the declaration of Papal infallibility accepted at Vatican I
(1869-70) had completed the work of defining the external structure of authority in the church, ordinary Catholics were now to
regard themselves as free to pursue their internal spiritual perfection as unique religious individuals.

Apparently innocent in itself, Hecker's pious counsel, when
rendered fully explicit by the encyclical, reveals the legion of "errors" that can be spawned by this "certain liberty": (1) external
spiritual direction tends to be neglected in favor of appeals to
immediate experience of the Holy Spirit; (2) natural virtues
tend to be praised to the detriment of the supernatural; (3) an
untenable distinction between active and passive virtue is asserted in order to denigrate humility, obedience, and absti-
nence; (4) the traditional religious life structured according to
solemn vows of poverty, chastity, and obedience, is unfairly
criticized for being out of touch with the spirit of the age; and (5)
an imprudent new way of approaching "those who differ with
us" is promoted at the expense of Catholic truth.[6] Whatever
their resonance in the vicissitudes of French Catholic
liberalism, these five particulars present a distorted account of
what Hecker hoped would be the eventual fruit of ordinary
Catholics cultivating their own authentic spirituality. In deny-

ing any connection with that "certain liberty" and the "errors" that it generates, perhaps Cardinal Gibbons protested our American innocence too much.

My thesis, then, is that *Testem benevolentiae* wasn't really about heresy at all. Americanism was never a challenge to Roman Catholic orthodoxy, as codified in the dogmas of the church, but an emerging style of religious praxis nurtured by the experience of Catholic people in America. This "certain liberty" that Leo XIII hoped to interdict was the fruit of a *Novus Ordo Seclorum,* the experimental "new order of the ages," to which the American revolution had given birth. In its explicitly religious implications, it is not shameful "indulgence" but, as Max Stackhouse has recently pointed out, "a liberation to new duty given by the grace of God, which leads to voluntary community, disciplined personal life, lay intellectuality, and social outreach." Indeed, as Leo XIII feared, this liberation is a liberation from the church; but he failed to grasp the Americanists' hope that such a liberation also occurs for the sake of the church. At stake in the "certain liberty" for which Americanists stand condemned is, in Stackhouse's terms, the revolutionary American principle of "self-governing association" and its extension to all the institutional sectors of society. America thus is an experiment in which "the basic, primordial freedom of the church to order its own life is taken as the basis for the organization of political, economic, educational, familial, and other aspects of life."[7]

Isaac Hecker's only "heresy" was to give Catholic expression to this, the original "American experiment in democracy." His "errors" consisted in drawing certain conclusions from this "new order of the ages" for the spiritual formation of a genuinely American Catholic laity. In Hecker's eyes, Catholicism promised to be God's chosen instrument for perfecting the habitual exercise of "intelligence and freedom" characteristic of the American civilization:

> I have the conviction that I can be all the better Cath-
> olic because I am an American: and all the better
> American because I am a Catholic.[8]

Elliott's *Life of Father Hecker,* of course, hightlighted many of
the features distinctive of the emerging style of American religious praxis. He dramatized its intensive awareness of the political, cultural, and religious history of the United States, especially as shaping the worldly mission of a truly American
Catholicism, and described as attractively as possible the
"manly" virtues common to all forms of American character and
community. His enthusiastic remarks in this area, no doubt pre-
cipitated the papal fears and triggered the Roman condemnation.

Whatever its role in *Testem benevolentiae,* Elliott's biography is to be treasured for what it tells us about Hecker's own
uniquely American appreciation of Catholicism. Like a back-
woods St. Justin Martyr, before his conversion Hecker had tried
and found wanting the various religious perspectives available
in America before the Civil War. Most significantly, he had come
to Brook Farm, conversed with Emerson and Thoreau, and, in
his own mind at least, had exhausted the possibilities of New
England transcendentalism. Yet along with the transcenden-
talists, Hecker also repudiated popular Calvinism. Its suicidal
doctrine of total depravity and its exclusive reliance on a sacred
Book for salvation were no substitute for personal religious experience. But for Hecker, Emerson, alas, was somewhat like
Moses: he could lead the sensitive soul to the promised land but
he couldn't actually take her across the river to the other side.
For transcendentalism lacked any sure test of discernment for
scrutinizing personal religious experience, and without such
critical scrutiny the American experiment in "self-governing association" was likely to fail. Hecker became a Catholic when he
discovered in Catholicism a principle of authority beyond the
autonomous self. It afforded him an affirmation of personal religious experience as intense as Emerson's own; but more than

that, it provided him with the key to free, associational living that transcendentalism lacked: the twofold activity of God the Holy Spirit, giving life to both the structures of community and the persons living faithfully by them. Improbable as it may seem, Hecker came to regard the presence of the Holy Spirit, as manifest in Catholic life and thought, as the key to discerning and thus fulfilling certain basic tendencies in the American character that transcendentalism could also discern but not fulfill.[9]

Though Elliott's biography labors mightily to make it understandable, Pope Leo's exposition of Hecker's "spiritual doctrine" completely ignores its irreducibly American context. Hecker's experimental approach to Catholic truth and the presence of the Holy Spirit within the community, though useful in disarming thoughtful Yankees, is dangerous because there's no telling what conclusions someone may draw from it. Never mind that neither Hecker nor his biographer ever asserted anything directly contradicting Catholic dogma; if allowed to stand, their naive invocation of the Holy Spirit could lead to unauthorized innovation in Catholic religious praxis. And such experimentation, even if undertaken for the best of motives, could hardly be tolerated by Rome.

Though Hecker thus may have had a decisive role in identifying the emerging style of American Catholic praxis and giving it a theological legitimacy, its condemnation was meant specifically as a warning to influential Americanists within the national hierarchy, notably John Ireland, John Keane, Denis O'Connell, and Cardinal Gibbons. Ireland's glowing introduction to the Hecker biography, in particular, provides the link between the crabbed bill of particulars found in *Testem benevolentiae* and their aspirations for an American Catholicism. For Ireland promoted the memory of Hecker as "a typical American priest," a man whose approach to Christian ministry was uniquely suited to the circumstances, both the opportunities and the trials, that Catholics encountered in this country. As if the distinctively Americanist flavor of Hecker's theology of the Holy

Spirit might go unrecognized, Ireland underscored its meaning as a principle of Catholic religious praxis:

> Each Christian soldier may take to the field, obeying the breathings of the Spirit of truth and piety within him, feeling that what he may do he should do. There is work for individual priests, and for individual laymen, and so soon as it is discovered let it be done. The responsibility is upon each one; the indifference of others is no excuse.[10]

For if, after Vatican I, "the need of repression had passed away," surely the Holy Spirit was prompting ordinary Catholics to discover the religious empowerment involved in feeling that what a person "may do he should do." Like Hecker, Ireland appreciated what experience taught about the benefits of encouraging a "certain liberty," even in the church.

Ireland's enthusiasm for his adopted homeland, and his hopeful vision of its future contribution to Western civilization, were generally shared by the Americanist bishops. Themselves Irish immigrants or the sons of immigrants, they readily identified with American democratic institutions and worked zealously to Americanize more recently arrived Catholics from other nations. Eventually they even endorsed the right of working people to organize themselves in labor unions, and did not allow foreign ecclesiastical scruples to stand in the way. Cardinal Gibbons, in particular, successfully defended Catholic participation in the Knights of Labor against other bishops bent on tarring them with the same brush reserved for European "secret societies."[11] The principle of self-governing association, so indispensable for empowering any community in America, was not to be sacrificed to the exigencies of papal statecraft.

Two incidents, in particular, dramatize the Americanist bishops' willingness to protect independent initiatives consistent with their own agenda. One is the controversial case of Fr. Edward McGlynn,[12] progressive New York pastor and pioneer

Catholic social activist, whose "new crusade" for economic justice anticipated the Protestant social gospel movement both in theory and in practice.[13] McGlynn used the economic analyses of Henry George, especially his socialist criticism of private property, to understand the poverty he encountered in the slums of New York. But when in 1886 he became politically active in George's unsuccessful campaign for mayor of New York, Archbishop Corrigan suspended McGlynn from the priesthood and issued a pastoral letter defending private property. Though McGlynn himself refused to cooperate with either Corrigan or the authorities in Rome appointed to judge his case, Cardinal Gibbons himself intervened to lift the excommunication of his fellow Americanist, pleading that the church must not be seen as the enemy of the poor. Later on, when Pope Leo XIII issued *Rerum novarum*, McGlynn felt that his "new crusade" had been vindicated even though the Papal encyclical did, at least in general terms, condemn socialism.

The other incident occurred in conjunction with the Chicago World's Fair of 1893. Here the issue is ecumenical, rather than political, activism. The Fair coincided with the World Parliament of Religions, a largely liberal Protestant attempt to celebrate the unity of the human race within the diversity of its religious traditions. The gathering, inspired by progressive ideals of world peace based ultimately on mutual religious understanding, listened to a series of addresses by major representatives of the various world religions. The addresses were refreshingly irenic in tone and strove not to perpetuate conventional apologetics, so often marred by *ad hominem* argument. Instead of rebuking Protestants and others for heresy, Bishop Keane, in an address drafted by Cardinal Gibbons, emphasized positively "The Needs of Humanity Supplied by the Catholic Religion." Its uncompromising social concern and liberating sense of spiritual mission ably carried on the legacy of Isaac Hecker.[14]

Though Gibbons and his Americanist colleagues had originally accepted the invitation to participate primarily for pragmatic reasons, the quality of their participation was heralded by many would-be ecumenists as opening "a new era in the history of the Catholic Church."[15] Such favorable notice, of course, did them little good among their enemies, either here or abroad. Praise from Protestants, infidels, and agnostics could only mean that the Americanists indeed were watering down the Catholic faith. The World Parliament of Religions could only be another way-station on the route to religious "indifferentism," that bugaboo of those who dread the possibility that "one religion is as good as another." Gibbons' reaction to such malicious distortion speaks well of his courage and loyalty to his colleagues. While he did everything in his power to reassure Rome, he used his considerable influence to protect those clerics, like Keane, who were identified with the World Parliament.

While neither of these incidents was decisive, each does illuminate the climate of opinion in which a Papal condemnation became both possible and, for some, desirable. When set against the background of increasing ethnic tension between Irish and German Catholics, and the smoldering discontent of the newer immigrants over the role of English language instruction in the Catholic schools, the issue of clerical participation in politics dramatized by McGlynn and the ecumenical adventure symbolized by the World Parliament of Religions, helped polarize Catholics in this country in relationship to the Americanist agenda. The American Catholic church's "search for self-identity" tended to get sidetracked in ethnic quarrels and clerical rivalries whose details need not be recounted here.[16] Suffice it to say that the Americanists helped bring on their own defeat by promoting their agenda in ways that belied it. Hopelessly mistaken about the "liberal" nature of Leo XIII's own sympathies, they presumptuously appealed to "higher authority" to suppress their "conservative" enemies. Their plotting backfired, of course, when the Vatican finally realized the implications of the Americanist agenda.

Once Rome took a stand with *Testem benevolentiae*, the Americanist influence slowly ebbed away. Even before the encyclical, O'Connell and Keane had been removed from their positions as rectors of the two most prominent centers of American priestly formation, the North American College in Rome and the Catholic University of America in Washington, D.C. Intellectually adventuresome journals, such as *The American Catholic Quarterly Review* and *The Catholic University Bulletin*, soon found themselves placed under a cloud of suspicion. After Pope Pius X's encyclical of 1907, *Pascendi*, condemned "Modernism," the finest of these journals, *The New York Review*, eventually was forced to stop publication. Like a hard frost in early spring, the ensuing intellectual chill that descended over the church made it certain that the Americanist agenda would have to wait another season before it would bear fruit.

Historians assure us that there is no direct connection between Americanism and what *Pascendi* condemned as "Modernism."[17] For Americanism was, and still is, "a certain liberty" in religious praxis, while "Modernism" was, and still is, a theoretical program for deconstructing orthodox Catholic dogma. To be self-consciously "Modernist" requires a degree of intellectual sophistication about history and hermeneutics that even the most theologically perceptive of the Americanists lacked. Americanism, by contrast, was not a program for systematic theology, but a new style of pastoral action based on openness to the experience of democracy. At the time of its repression, it was seeking, and still seeks, articulation in a theory, a practical theology if you will, capable of generating critical reflection on this praxis. Owning up to the Americanist heresy means, among other things, working to create the appropriate practical theology.[18]

In the aftermath of the Papal condemnations, however, American Catholicism remained American mostly in its anti-intellectualism.[19] An unprecedented dread of heresy and innovation spread like cancer phobia within American Catholic institutions, especially the colleges and seminaries. Even the educated clergy soon became so demoralized that adult conversation with the emerging American civilization was nearly impossible. Nevertheless, this anti-intellectualism retained a distinctively Catholic flavor. Bald assertions of intellectual superiority which, of course, were not open to challenge, consoled American Catholics for their failure to generate research contributing to the development of any field of inquiry, with the possible exception of religious social ethics. The alleged immutability of Catholic dogma became an excuse for intellectual sloth. As Thomas Gannon captures it, such ignorance masked itself as merely logical: "For you cannot be a possessor of truth and a pursuer of truth at one and the same time."[20] The Americanists, as well as Modernists in Europe, had committed the unpardonable sin of admitting that experience contained truths the Catholic church has yet to learn. Repentance lay in confessing the opposite opinion: *Nihi novi sub sole* ("nothing's new under the sun"). By the eve of World War I the American Catholic church thus had entered into the long dark night of its largely self-imposed exile from the mainstream of American culture.

In spite of the papal condemnations, World War I and its aftermath provided challenges and opportunities in which the Americanist style of religious praxis continued to grow. The general mobilization for World War I required the development of national organizations capable of, and comfortable with, broadly ecumenical patterns of interdenominational cooperation. Unlike the World Parliament of Religions, in purpose these organizations were entirely pragmatic: they were to rally patriotic support for the American war effort among the diverse religious and ethnic communities of this country. Thus was formed, first, the National Catholic War Council, and later in peacetime, the National Catholic Welfare Council, which after some future skirmishing with the Vatican became the National Catholic Welfare Conference.[21] Working within the scope of these organizations' unprecedented commitment to social and political action, the American Catholic church continued to struggle with the tension between its institutional loyalty to Rome and its inescapable involvement in our national experience. The social and political nature of the Welfare Council's mission, and the way in which it was organized and adminis-

tered, virtually guaranteed that the experiences that had originally generated the Americanist vision, especially the practice
and principle of self-governing association, would continue like
a subterranean spring to stimulate the development of authentically American Catholicism.

The first of the Welfare Council's fruits, the celebrated
"Bishops' Program of Social Reconstruction" authored by John
A. Ryan in 1919, bears witness indirectly to both the continuing
vitality of the Americanist agenda and the trauma resulting
from its repression. Without so much as a nod to its precedents
in the struggles of turn of the century radicals like McGlynn, the
"Bishops' Program" tried to take advantage of the "teachable
moment" that the Great War had created for both victors and
vanquished alike. Insisting that "the only safeguard of peace is
social justice," it reviews other proposals addressing the virtually universal unrest following the war and puts its weight
squarely behind piecemeal reformism. True to the Americanist
agenda, it advocates policies based either on the experience of
the federal agencies managing U.S. industrial mobilization during the war, or on pending legislation drafted in light of that experience. Yet even so, its unambiguous commitment to economic
justice for all Americans, especially "the weaker sections of the
working class,"[22] means that, despite its repudiation of
socialism as impractical in the American context, the "Program's" critics and some of its admirers would still regard it as
socialistic. At its best, then, the "Bishops' Program" represents
the blend of pragmatism and moral idealism that had characterized earlier Americanist attempts to create a Catholic social
gospel.

When compared with the work of its Americanist predecessors, what the "Program" lacks is style. The exuberant self-con-
fidence is gone; the generous patriotism based on a common
sense of gratitude for this nation's revolutionary promise is mis-
sing; and there's no hint of the intellectual excitement involved
in contributing to the American experiment in democracy. A
case in point is the "Program's" treatment of Leo XIII's *Rerum*

novarum, a Papal encyclical on the condition of the working class, that was to achieve almost mythic status as the alleged inspiration for modern Catholic social teaching. Like other statements of Catholic principle, the encyclical merits only one explicit, though very nebulous, reference. Faithfully mirroring conditions in the American Catholic church which it represented, the "Bishops' Program" thus tries to avoid theological controversy by being tough-mindedly pragmatic in matters of policy and tightlipped, though authoritative, about Catholic social teaching. For all its farsighted policy recommendations, the "Bishops' Program" couldn't help reflecting the intellectual poverty of an American Catholic church now speaking to the nation from spiritual exile.

More telling evidence of the unacknowledged trauma inflicted by the Vatican's repression of the Americanist heresy may be found in a popular college textbook written for the Department of Social Action of the National Catholic Welfare Conference by the same John A. Ryan and a Jesuit, Moorhouse F. X. Millar.[23] First published in 1922, *The State and the Church* provides a compendium of Catholic social teaching on church-state relations, based primarily on another, less celebrated encyclical of Pope Leo XIII, *Immortale Dei* (1885). Ryan's commentary on the encyclical doggedly defends its "hard sayings," that is, its insistence that the state make "a public profession of religion," its claim that the Catholic church be granted favored status in law, and its principle of intolerance toward anything it regards as error.[24] Using every technique known in the art of interpreting papal encyclicals, Ryan tries to sugarcoat these hard sayings for an American audience. At no point does he suggest that American Catholicism may have an equally legitimate, though differing view, of church-state relations.[25] At no point is he moved to defend the American experiment in self-governing association.

Ryan's docility, however, stands in curious contrast to two Americanist essays included at the end of the same book, one by John Ireland on "Catholicism and Americanism" and the other by John Lancaster Spalding on "Patriotism." Ireland's essay, in particular, couldn't be further from Ryan's commentary either in style or in substance. Here is Ireland's ringing defense of that "certain liberty" in America:

> Necessarily religious freedom is the basic life of America, the cement running through all its walls and battlements, the safeguard of its peace and prosperity. Violate religious freedom against Catholics: Our swords are at once unsheathed. Violate it in favor of Catholics against non-Catholics: No less readily do they leap from the scabbard. [26]

Ireland's essay, however, comes from the years prior to World War I, before the big chill had fully set in. Voices like his were not to be heard again in the American church until John Courtney Murray reopened these same issues during World War II.

Once again it was America's wartime experience of "intercreedal cooperation" that helped rekindle the Americanist controversy.[27] Murray's attempts to defend American Catholic participation in the National Conference of Christians and Jews provoked reactionaries like Joseph C. Fenton who predictably accused him of "indifferentism." Also predictably, the teachings of Pope Leo XIII, including *Testem benevolentiae*, were invoked in order to silence Murray for falling once more into the unpardonable sin of learning from our American experience. Murray responded by reformulating the practical problem of ecumenical participation as a question of historical method in theology. Thus under extreme pressure from both critics at home and their allies in Rome, Murray quietly laid the foundations for the American theological revolution that achieved a momentary triumph in Vatican II's *Declaration on Religious Freedom*.[28] Owning up to the Americanist heresy will remain a nostalgic fantasy unless we pause to consider briefly the nature of Murray's theological achievement.

The issue, which *Testem benevolentiae* had skirted in condemning a "certain liberty" in the church, boils down to whether Catholic life and thought can undergo historical development. Like Isaac Hecker, Murray insisted that it necessarily must as Catholicism becomes incarnate in a variety of cultures. In light of such development the Catholic theologian's task is to "vindicate the internal consistency of Catholic doctrine at any given moment" by formulating the perennial "principles"[29] operative in the new perspectives. The theologian thus can "show forth the fact that development has been truly organic."[30] Like the Americanists before him, Murray denied that such a view of theological development would lead to watering down Catholic teaching or that it was an expediency motivated by the "liberal spirit." Responding to Fenton's accusations, he artfully defended his view as consistent with even the teachings of Leo XIII.[31] *Testem benevolentiae*, Murray magnanimously argued, was not meant to deny the obvious relativities of historical development, but to warn against those forms of cultural adaptation that might somehow compromise the "deposit of faith."[32]

Fenton, however, rejected Murray's view of the theologian's task. Promoting historical development by defining certain "principles" of continuity struck Fenton as reductionistic. Narrowing the focus of his dispute with Murray, he insisted that theologians were not free to depart from the "technical historical terms" that had become authoritative in Catholic tradition. Theologians could not regard these terms as historically "contingent," as Murray allegedly did, in order to diminish their authority for judging current development in Catholic life and thought. Once they had been "integrated into the dogmatic formulae of the Church," they were to be considered as immutable as the "deposit of faith" itself.[33] In this narrower form, Fenton's position amounted to an "integralism," that is, an illusory claim to orthodoxy based on the mistaken belief that one's own perspective preserves the whole of Catholic tradition, irreconcilable in principle with Murray's view.

This dispute over theological method, of course, did not occur in a vacuum. Murray's defense of the legitimacy of historical development in Catholic life and thought was specifically designed to break the intellectual strait jacket in which American Catholics found themselves over church-state relations. Rather than acquiesce, as John A. Ryan had, in the "hard sayings" of Leo XIII's *Immortale Dei*, Murray hoped to distinguish between the perennial Catholic "principles" implicit in the encyclical's teaching and the historical contingencies governing their specific reformulation in turn of the century Europe. Along with earlier generations of Americanists, Murray acknowledged the perennial validity of the church's distinctive mission in the world, and insisted that this mission was not to be confused with that of the state. Some European states may have honored this distinction by accepting certain "concordats" granting a special legal status to the Catholic church. But another set of historical circumstances may legitimately give rise to different arrangements; for example, the American experiment in self-governing association may require a stricter separation of church and state. Murray's theological method, in short, served to protect the integrity of Catholic religious praxis in "a state organized on the constitutional and political lines proper to the tradition of Anglo-American democracy."[34]

Echoing Hecker's own insights, Murray insisted that America's democratic ethos was different from the anticlerical republicanism characteristic of Continental Europe. American Catholicism had been shaped by its distinctive experience of democracy. Participating in the American experiment had given the church "a new kind of spiritual existence, not tasted on the Continent, — the experience of reliance on its own inner resources." The question for Murray was whether "the Church in America [is] to be allowed to travel her own historical path . . . , remaining faithful to essential Catholic principle . . . , [or] is [she] to repudiate the history of America in what is most unique about it — its installation of a political tradition sharply in contrast with that of modern Continental Europe?"[35]

On this issue, Murray clearly stood with his Americanist predecessors in defending "a certain liberty," and in doing so on a more explicitly theological level he deepened our understanding of its implications for American Catholicism.

Not until Vatican II, however, was Murray's Americanist approach to theology and church-state relations finally, if perhaps only momentarily, accepted by the Catholic church as a whole. This is not the place to celebrate once more the story of Murray's rehabilitation by the American bishops and his crucial role in drafting the Council's *Declaration on Religious Freedom*. In recognizing a human right to religious liberty, this Declaration endorsed the spirit animating the American principle of separation of church and state, claiming as essential to human dignity that inviolable liberty of conscience which is given constitutional protection here. What had been condemned at the turn of the century as heresy now seemed to enjoy the privileged status of orthodoxy. Yet Murray himself knew that Vatican II was only a beginning in American Catholicism's new springtime. Commenting on the *Declaration on Religious Freedom*, he noted that, while it did recognize religious pluralism for society as a whole in the name of freedom of conscience, it lacked a similar appreciation for religious freedom within the church. Nearly twenty years after Murray's death, American Catholicism has conducted all sorts of experiments testing the limits and possibilities of that freedom, but it still lacks a theology reflecting the impact of American experience upon the church.

My contention is that such a theology is unlikely to emerge until American Catholicism owns up to the Americanist heresy. The history of the American church over the past century has been decisively influenced by Americanism in her youthful enthusiasm for it, in her embarrassed denials of any association with it, and, more recently, in her halting attempts to recover it as part of the church's historic identity. Repressing the heresy any longer is neither possible nor desirable. In an era when all religious communities must observe what Peter Berger once called "the heretical imperative,"[36] American Catholicism is fortunate in having once been innovative enough and daring enough to choose its own past as a guide to its future. After spending so many years trying to live down the Americanist heresy, perhaps it is time for American Catholics to begin living up to it.

What, then, is the "principle" — to use Murray's word — at stake in the Americanist heresy? What makes it significant beyond the historical contingencies of its original condemnation? Pope Leo XIII prophetically discerned the truth of it when he warned of the danger of introducing "a certain liberty" into the church. Yet as this attempt to create a "dangerous memory" may suggest, this "certain liberty" is not something fully realized either in the aspirations and achievements of the original Americanists, beginning with Hecker, or in the reopening of the American Catholic church's "search for self-identity" after Vatican II. Rather, it is manifest in the consistent tendency of Catholics to define their own integrity in terms of this nation's ongoing experiment in "self-governing association." In this sense the Americanist heresy is rooted in the very foundations of Christianity in this country, a heritage common to the whole spectrum of American Protestant and Catholic communities of faith. It has become, and inevitably must become, the agenda for American Catholicism, whenever Catholic people consider fully the logic of their circumstances here — how it is that their habitual patterns of organizing themselves for participation in our common life are religiously significant.

Whatever the Pope may have feared in this "certain liberty," would-be Americanists continue to embrace it, not as a pretext for doing your own thing, but as an invitation to do the Catholic thing without being coerced. Clergy and laity will no longer relate to each other as shepherds and sheep, despite the weight of these images in traditional Christian iconography. All persons, whether exalted or humble in ecclesial status, are to participate to the fullest in the common work of the church, contributing whatever unique perspectives their individual histories may generate, confident of the presence of the Holy Spirit, not just in the church to which they are loyal, but also in their own experience — to which they must also be faithful. Americanism, in other words, is the dream of a religious community born to genuine freedom, one in which diversity is not a threat but an occasion for cooperation.

Had Isaac Hecker been given the opportunity to name this "principle," he probably would have called it Paulinism. For surely it does resonate with the ecclesiology that Paul the Apostle describes in his Letters, especially those addressed to the Christians in Corinth: "There is a variety of gifts but always the same Spirit . . . " (1 Cor. 12:1). Yet Hecker would not have objected to the label, Americanism, because he had rediscovered this Pauline understanding of Christian pluralism in an ethos of democratic institutions that so naturally supported the distinctive virtues of his fellow citizens. Catholicism was flourishing in this pluralistic democratic ethos, and Hecker regarded this unexpected development as providential. Almost a century later Murray was much more cautious: Thomas Jefferson's agrarian republic had long since been transformed by urbanization and industrialization, massive social dislocations themselves accompanied by still more massive waves of Catholic immigration. The democratic ethos still celebrated by Murray had become less a natural result of American institutions and more a matter of deliberate, though often tenuous, conviction. In such historical circumstances, Murray could see American Catholicism renewing the democratic ethos as once that ethos had inspired renewal in the church.

In our current situation, if the American Catholic bishops are to join their people in owning up to the Americanist heresy, they must identify themselves once more with the kind of national episcopal leadership exemplified by Gibbons, Ireland, Spalding, and Keane, and encourage — beyond anything ever dreamed by these bishops — further institutional experiment and theological development along the paths envisioned by Hecker and Murray. It will not do simply to bring more quotes from these sources into their pastoral letters. Juxtaposing material culled from papal encyclicals with statements from these leading Americanists would only transfer to them, and thus perpetuate, the mystique of Roman authoritarianism from which they only partially succeeded in liberating the church. The Americanists can be taken as authoritative only to the extent that their agenda inspires Catholics today — clergy as well as laity — to make similar efforts. For remembering the Americanist heresy is and ought to remain a liberating activity.

How might the American bishops keep alive this dangerous memory in their pastoral letters? While I have other, more substantive suggestions to make later on, here let me insist upon a point of theological method. The bishops can stop perpetuating the myth that Catholic social teaching is a single, harmonious tradition of faithful response to the initiatives of the modern papacy. The recent pastoral letters on war and peace and the economy, I believe, have begun to move in the right direction, but very hesitantly. Stated positively, the bishops and their advisers need to go further, when presenting their overviews of Catholic social teaching, in honestly acknowledging distinctively American contributions to their understanding of the tradition, whether those contributions stem from saints or sinners, prophets or heretics, Catholic or nonCatholic.[37]

Two examples from the pastoral letter on war and peace may help clarify both the right direction and the hesitation that remain typical of the bishops' current leadership. The first is taken from the letter's discussion of Christian nonviolence and pacifism.[38] After having reaffirmed the primacy of the just war tradition in Catholic social teaching, the letter gratefully acknowledges that "the nonviolent witness of such figures as Dorothy Day and Martin Luther King has had a profound impact upon the life of the Church in the United States." Though the assertion is true, it is a masterpiece of understatement. For apart from the historic witness of these two modern prophets, the one a Catholic laywoman, the other a Protestant minister, it would be difficult to account for the differences separating the

American bishops' interpretation of the just war tradition from those offered by, say, the pastoral letters of the French and German bishops. Not that Christian pacifism has become the dominant perspective of the American bishops, but their openness to the arguments of nuclear pacifists would be inconceivable apart from the witness of Day and King, and the many American Catholic activists whom their teachings have inspired.

Indeed, so great has been their influence that the American bishops broke new ground in acknowledging a pluralism of legitimate moral perspectives in the tradition of Catholic social teaching on war and peace. This full paragraph taken from the pastoral letter bears repeating:

> Both [just war teaching and non-violence] find their roots in the Christian theological tradition; each contributes to the full moral vision we need in pursuit of a human peace. We believe the two perspectives support and complement one another, each preserving the other from distortion. Finally in an age of technological warfare, analysis from the viewpoint of non-violence and analysis from the viewpoint of the just war teaching often converge and agree in their opposition to methods of warfare which are in fact indistinguishable from total warfare.[39]

Nor are the bishops surprised by this convergence. For their historical interpretation of the tradition has located, in a manner that Murray himself might have appreciated, a Catholic principle underlying both perspectives: "a common presumption against the use of force as a means of settling disputes." Surely, in this example, the bishops are moving in the right direction, at least methodologically. Consistent with the Americanist agenda, they are remaining open to the experiences of people in this country, Catholics and nonCatholics alike, and are allowing that experience to reshape the contours of traditional Catholic social teaching.

The other example, involving a narrow comparison of the second and third drafts of the same pastoral letter, illustrates the hesitation that keeps the bishops from fully acknowledging their Americanist heritage. Evidence of its lingering repression can be discovered in the letter's discussion of Catholic social teaching on nuclear deterrence.[40] The second draft implies not only that there has been doctrinal development on this issue, but also that the American bishops themselves rightly have been at the forefront of this development. It pointedly suggests that beyond all the possible consequences of a policy of nuclear deterrence, there is a difficult problem in the morality of even threatening to use nuclear weapons. They repeat a principle asserted in their neglected pastoral letter of 1976, "To Live in Christ Jesus": "As possessors of a vast nuclear arsenal, we must also be aware that not only is it wrong to attack civilian populations but it is also wrong to threaten to attack them as part of a strategy of deterrence."[41] They reinforce this principle by quoting at length Cardinal John Krol's testimony, on behalf of the United States Catholic Conference, supporting the ratification of the SALT II Treaty. Here is the gist of it:

> As long as there is hope of this [nuclear disarmament] occurring, Catholic moral teaching is willing, while negotiations proceed, to tolerate the possession of nuclear weapons for deterrence as the lesser of two evils. If that hope were to disappear, the moral attitude of the Catholic church would certainly have to shift to one of uncompromising condemnation of both use and possession of such weapons.

The second draft then goes on to support this interpretation of the moral "paradox" of nuclear deterrence by referring to Pope John Paul II's address in June of 1982 to the United Nations Second Special Session on Disarmament.

The third and final drafts of the pastoral letter, however, give only passing reference to the 1976 letter, "To Live in Christ

Jesus," and omit the passage just cited from their quotation of Cardinal Krol's testimony. The moral problem involved in threatening nuclear war, so provocatively opened up in the second draft, now gets submerged as the letter's discussion of nuclear deterrence concentrates on a more detailed exposition of the Papal address. In the the third and final drafts, the "paradox" of deterrence seems attenuated, and the ultimatum implied in Cardinal Krol's demand for serious negotiations definitely has disappeared. Admittedly, both the earlier and the later drafts come down on the issue more or less in the same position, arguing for a "strictly conditioned moral acceptance of nuclear deterrence" as negotiations continue.[42] But the moral tone resonating from the position is different.

What accounts for the change between the later and the earlier drafts? In January 1983, key members of the bishops' drafting committee had been summoned to Rome for a meeting with high Vatican officials and representatives of the Catholic hierarchies of Western Europe. This notorious meeting did not, as the *National Catholic Reporter* (February 11, 1983) erroneously indicated, give the American bishops a "green light . . . to take the nuclear morality wherever it may go." Instead, it raised a series of formidable objections to the pastoral letter, ranging from a general challenge to the right of national bishops' conferences to issue pastoral letters to specific points of Biblical exegesis. The memoranda issued after the meeting indicated that Cardinal Casaroli, who had delivered the Papal address to the United Nations the previous June, provided the American bishops with a personal tutorial on the Pope's view of nuclear deterrence. The drafting committee could not have failed to catch the hint: they dare not be more Catholic than the Pope in dramatizing the "paradox" of nuclear deterrence.

There are several other issues raised by that meeting that will have to be addressed before a theology adequate to the church's "New American Experiment in Democracy" can be developed. For the moment, though, I wish to emphasize the problem that Vatican interventions like this one create for the American bishops and their fellow citizens who look to them for guidance.

On the one hand, a comparison of the earlier and later drafts may suggest that the bishops capitulated to another Roman intrigue, bent on repressing one more Catholic attempt to learn from American experience. The second draft did not contradict Papal teaching, but it did reformulate the principle at stake in that teaching with an urgency demanded at that time by the circumstances of American public opinion. Nevertheless, since even this deviation was too much for the watchdogs of the Vatican, the bishops quietly withdrew it from the third and final drafts.

On the other hand, the same comparison of drafts may suggest that, in light of the strategic objections raised at that meeting, the very fact that the pastoral letter emerged as substantially intact as it did attests to the drafting committee's subtle but tenacious leadership. Cardinal Joseph Bernadin and his associates prudently chose to protect the pastoral letter project by not confronting the Vatican. On either reading, however, having taken once more the insider's path of ecclesiastical diplomacy, the bishops risk leaving their fellow Americans — Catholic and Protestant alike — with doubts about the decisiveness of their moral leadership.

In light of our openly dangerous memory of the Americanist tradition, this episode, though hardly surprising, raises once more the question of American Catholicism's unresolved ambivalence about the principle and practice of self-governing association. No doubt, the American church will continue to struggle with this principle for as long as it faithfully lives its Catholic identity. Remembering the Americanist heresy will not resolve the struggle, but it should encourage all American Catholics to accept their part in that struggle, fortified by a proud tradition of patriotic visionaries who understood that their love for this country and its institutions could not help but transform the way they approached each other in the presence of the Holy Spirit. The truly liberating character of the Americanist memory will be discovered, not in the bitter contemplation of an almost forgotten condemnation, but in our hopeful participation in creating the next stage of the American experiment in democracy.

Notes

1. The concept of "dangerous memory" is adapted from the work of Johannes Metz. Cf. especially Metz's essay, "The Future in the Memory of Suffering," in *Faith in History and Society: Toward a Practical Fundamental Theology* (New York: The Seabury Press, 1980), pp. 100-118.

2. *Documents of American Catholic History*, John Tracy Ellis, ed. (Milwaukee: Bruce Publishing, 1956), p. 553.

3. "Pope Leo XIII's Encyclical *Testem benevolentiae* on Americanism, January 22, 1899," *ibid.*, p. 554.

4. *Ibid.*, p. 555.

5. *Ibid.*, p. 556.

6. *Ibid.*, pp. 557-561.

7. Max Stackhouse, *Creeds, Society, and Human Rights: A Study in Three Civilizations* (Grand Rapids, Michigan: William B. Eerdmans, 1984), p. 57.

8. As quoted in David J. O'Brien's essay, "An Evangelical Imperative: Isaac Hecker, Catholicism, and Modern Society," in *Hecker Studies: Essays on the Thought of Isaac Hecker*, John Farina, ed. (Ramsey, New Jersey: Paulist Press, 1983), p. 106.

9. Cf. Walter Elliott, *The Life of Father Hecker* (New York: The Columbus Press, 1894); and John C. Farina, *An American Experience of God: The Spirituality of Isaac Hecker* (New York: Paulist Press, 1981).

10. John Ireland, "Introduction" to Walter Elliott, *op. cit.*, pp. xv-xvi.

11. Cf. "Cardinal Gibbons' Defense of the Knights of Labor (February 20, 1887)," in Ellis, ed., *op. cit.*, pp. 460-473.

12. For Hecker's negative reactions to McGlynn's defiance, see O'Brien, *art. cit.*, p. 115.

13. James Hennesey, S.J., *American Catholics: A History of the Roman Catholic Community in the United States* (New York: Oxford University Press, 1981), pp. 189, 197.

14. James Cardinal Gibbons, "The Needs of Humanity Supplied by the Catholic Religion," in *The Catholic World, Vol. LVIII, No. 343* (October, 1893), pp. 1-9.

15. John Tracy Ellis, *The Life of James Cardinal Gibbons, Archbishop of Baltimore, 1834-1921*, Two Volumes (Milwaukee: Bruce Publishing, 1952), p. 2:17-20.

16. Cf. Hennesey, *op. cit.*, pp. 184-203; cf. Jay Dolan, *The American Catholic Experience: A History from Colonial Times to the Present* (Garden City, New York: Doubleday, 1985), pp. 294-333.

17. Cf. Michael V. Gannon, "Before and After Modernism: The Intellectual Isolation of the American Priest," in John Tracy Ellis, ed., *The Catholic Priest in the United States: Historical Investigations* (Collegeville, Minnesota: St. John's University Press, 1977), pp. 337f.

18. Cf. Dennis P. McCann and Charles R. Strain, *Polity and Praxis: A Program for American Practical Theology* (Minneapolis, Minnesota: Winston Press/ Seabury Books, 1985).

19. Cf. Richard Hofstadter, *Anti-Intellectualism in American Life* (New York: Vintage Books/Random House, 1963).

20. Gannon, *art. cit.*, p. 358.

21. Cf. Ellis, ed., *Documents of American Catholic History*, pp. 629-35.

22. *Ibid.*, p. 614.

23. Hennesey, *op. cit.*, p. 251.

24. John A. Ryan and Moorhouse F. X. Millar, *The State and the Church*, written and edited for the Department of Social Action of the National Catholic Welfare Council. (New York: Macmillan, 1922), pp. 29-39.

25. In all fairness to Ryan and Millar, the position that they argued had become virtually mandatory after the first encyclical of Leo XIII specifically addressed to the church in the United States, *Longinquam oceani* (1895). Cf. Ellis, ed., *Documents of American Catholic History*, pp. 514-27.

26. Ryan and Millar, *op. cit.*, p. 288.

27. Donald E. Pelotte, *John Courtney Murray: Theologian in Conflict* (New York: Paulist Press, 1976), pp. 141-77.

28. Cf. *Declaration on Religious Freedom (Dignitatis Humanae)*. In Walter M. Abbott, ed., *The Documents of Vatican II* (London: Geoffrey Chapman, 1967), pp. 675-697.

29. Pelotte, *op. cit.*, p. 156.

30. *Ibid.*, p. 166.

31. Cf. *Testem benevolentiae* in Ellis, ed., *Documents of American Catholic History*, p. 555. For another view of Murray's attempt to ground his Americanism in Catholic natural law theory, see Charles E. Curran, *Directions in Catholic Social Ethics* (Notre Dame, Indiana: University of Notre Dame Press, 1985), pp. 93-100.

32. Pelotte, *op. cit.*, p. 157.

33. *Ibid.*, p. 162.

34. *Ibid.*, p. 167.

35. Cf. John Courtney Murray's "Introduction" to the *Declaration on Religious Freedom (Dignitatis Humanae)*, in Abbott, ed., *op. cit.*, p. 674.

36. Peter Berger, *The Heretical Imperative: Contemporary Possibilities of Religious Affirmation* (Garden City, New York: Anchor Books/Doubleday, 1979), p. 28.

37. Cf. Curran, *op. cit.*, pp. 71-104.

38. National Conference of Catholic Bishops, *The Challenge of Peace: God's Promise and Our Response* (Washington, D.C.: United States Catholic Conference, 1983), par. 111-21.

39. *Ibid.*, par. 121.

40. For a different view of the moral arguments on the "paradox" of nuclear deterrence, see Curran, *op. cit.*, pp. 187-94.

41. National Conference of Catholic Bishops, "The Challenge of Peace: The Second Draft," in the *National Catholic Reporter* (November 5, 1982), p. 15.

42. National Conference of Catholic Bishops, *op. cit.*, par. 186.

2

THE FORBIDDEN FRUIT OF COLLEGIALITY: LOOKING BACK AT "CALL TO ACTION"

The task of giving life to the principles of Catholic social teaching is not a mechanical task of applying
ready-made solutions to fixed situations. The passage from principle to practice involves both a testing
of the situation by the principle and a testing of the
teachings by the demands of concrete and complex
problems.

— J. Bryan Hehir, "Introduction" to the National
Conference of Catholic Bishops' *Liberty and Justice
for All: A Discussion Guide*

Remembering the Americanist heresy is dangerous only if
the memory can be connected to the actual lived experience of
Catholics today. But in order to establish this point of connection between the Americanist heresy and our aspirations for the
church's "New Experiment in Democracy," we must savor once
again the forbidden fruit of Vatican II. Like the tree of life in the
Garden of Eden, Vatican II offered Catholics worldwide the
prospect of knowing good and evil. Our eyes were opened, in this
country as in so many others, when the whole People of God
tasted the forbidden fruit of collegiality. What had been reserved only to the Pope and the bishops now became part of the
experience of ordinary Catholics struggling to discern the meaning of their Christian faith in an all-too-precarious world. Once
the fruit had been eaten we could no longer comfort ourselves
with blissful illusions of orthodoxy.

37

It is providential that Vatican II coincided with the home-coming of American Catholics from our largely self-imposed spiritual exile. Encouraged by the massive popularity of the young Catholic President and the old Catholic Pope with young ideas, John F. Kennedy and Pope John XXIII, Catholics were re-discovering America and participating once again in the na-tion's public life with a freshness that disarmed both their sym-pathizers and critics. The Council's decrees, beginning with the *Constitution on the Sacred Liturgy*, which authorized the use of vernacular languages including English in the Mass, and cul-minating in the *Declaration on Religious Freedom*, were taken by many as permission to experiment with virtually all aspects of American Catholic life and thought. In light of the issues raised by our attempt to own up to the Americanist heresy, how-ever, we must restrict our focus to how Vatican II prepared the way for Catholicism's "New Experiment in Democracy." How is it that the work of the Council opened our eyes and stirred our desire for renewing the church according to perennially Amer-ican practices of "self-governing association"?

The forbidden fruit, I contend, is contained in Vatican II's call for "collegiality" within the church. A century earlier, just after Vatican I, Isaac Hecker had reluctantly accepted that Council's definition of papal primacy and infallibility as com-pleting the external structure of authority within the church. Whether or not Hecker had been as foolish in trying to em-phasize the Holy Spirit's presence in ordinary believers as *Tes-tem benevolentiae* later declared him to be, he certainly proved wrong on the institutional question. For the actions taken by the worldwide assembly of Catholic bishops gathered at Vatican II in effect declared that Vatican I had left unfinished business: the definition of Papal authority had to be completed, in its turn, by a rethinking of the role of both the clergy, starting with the bishops, and the laity in church governance. The result was an epoch-making change in Catholic ecclesiology, whose implica-tions have yet to be fully appreciated.

Initially, "collegiality" may seem like a very unpromising

kind of forbidden fruit. For it literally refers to the fact that the Catholic bishops as a whole constitute a "college," which has its authority in the church by virtue of apostolic succession. Theirs is a shared authority, derived from the episcopal ministry that they have inherited as a body, in an unbroken succession linking them ultimately, according to Catholic dogma, with Jesus' twelve apostles. While Catholic tradition gives countless examples of bishops exercising collegial authority, notably in the Ecumenical Councils of the church, "collegiality" became a theological problem only during the later Middle Ages, when in response to the chronic weakness of the Roman papacy certain canonists tried to assert the authority of such Councils over the Pope. This "Conciliarism," forcibly repressed whenever the papacy was strong enough to reassert itself, was formally condemned at Vatican I. Vatican II, however, tried to affirm the new collegiality while denying the old Conciliarism by insisting on the essential unity of the bishops and the Pope: "Together with its head, the Roman Pontiff, and never without its head, the episcopal order is the subject of supreme and full power over the universal Church."[1] This formula, however, remains innocent about possible conflicts between the body of bishops and its head, but that innocence was quickly dispelled as soon as all concerned experienced a taste of collegiality in practice.

As soon as the focus shifts — as inevitably it must — from theory to praxis, or from dogma to experience, "collegiality" becomes a symbol legitimating experimentation with the kinds of institutional structures in which it can actually be exercised. It is the new Catholic religious praxis emerging in these structures, and not some abstract theses dubbed Conciliarism, that, given the American environment of "self-governing association," allowed the forbidden fruit to work its beneficial effects. For once the principles of uncoerced participation, public discussion,and open consensus formation become part of the deliberative processes of the bishops, these same principles will begin to shape the institutional routines through which they exercise their authority of whatever sort, over clergy and laity, and in

matters of doctrine as well as discipline. After Vatican II, in
short, American Catholic bishops should no longer be regarded
as innocent when it comes to experimenting with democracy
within the church. The massive opportunity afforded by the
Council to experience collegiality firsthand[2] is what distinguishes today's bishops from even the most farsighted of their
Americanist predecessors.

This is especially true of their experience here with the National Conference of Catholic Bishops. Though the American
bishops may have had little role in cultivating Vatican II's tree
of knowledge, certainly they were poised to taste its fruit even
before the ink was dry on the Council's decrees. The National
Catholic Welfare Conference, and the bishops' generally successful collegial experience with it since World War I, gave them
an institutional base from which to create the national "episcopal conference" mandated in the decrees of Vatican II. These
decrees so far surpass the hopes of the Americanists who had
struggled to gain and retain Vatican approval for the Welfare
Conference that not only do they give the new structure pastoral
responsibility for "programs of the apostolate which are fittingly
adapted to the circumstances of the age,"[3] but also juridical authority over "regulation of the liturgy within certain defined
limits."[4] In order to implement these and other Conciliar decrees, the American bishops in 1966 reorganized themselves to
practice collegiality in "a two tiered arrangement," the National
Conference of Catholic Bishops (N.C.C.B.) and the United
States Catholic Conference (U.S.C.C.).[5]

It would be a mistake, nevertheless, to think of the church's
"New Experiment" as simply a revolution from above, a series of
administrative reforms initiated by the N.C.C.B. and the
U.S.C.C. For at the same time that the bishops were experimenting with collegiality among themselves, clergy and laity
were undertaking a wholesale renovation of Catholic life and
thought based on a newly acquired taste for participatory democracy. Priests' senates and parish councils, only the most institutionalized of these associations, began to interact with lay

organizations in ways that promised to distribute the fruit of collegiality throughout the whole People of God. These local structures soon gave rise to increasingly formal networks, like the National Federation of Priests' Councils and the National Assembly of Women Religious, which mediate between the grass roots level and the national episcopal conference. Often resisted at first, these and a host of other associations within the church soon were actively collaborating with the bishops' organizations in consultative processes that are the best examples of the rebirth of an Americanist Catholicism.

The most telling example of this virtually spontaneous recovery of that "certain liberty" for which the Americanists struggled is the "Call to Action" consultation organized by the N.C.C.B.'s Committee for the Observance of the U.S. Bicentennial. This process, extending over two years and involving, in one way or another, virtually every Catholic organization in America, culminated in the controversial "Call to Action" conference, held in Detroit in October of the Bicentennial year, 1976. I wish to use the "Call to Action" process and the controversy inspired by it as a model, not only in order to understand some aspects of the recent pastoral letters' approach to Catholic social teaching, but also in order to anticipate the problems likely to occur if the church seriously involves itself in a "New Experiment in Democracy." Both of these concerns will raise theological questions regarding the nature of a Catholic religious praxis oriented to the principle of "self-governing association," questions whose answers will be worked out in later chapters of this book.

Perhaps because of the controversy surrounding it, "Call to Action" has not merited so much as a single mention in either of the recent pastoral letters. Yet alongside the Americanist heresy, it stands as a dangerous memory precisely because it gives authentic witness to the hopes of ordinary American Catholics, unashamed of the knowledge that is theirs because of Vatican II. Furthermore, the embarrassment that the "Call to Action" conference caused for certain prominent leaders in the

N.C.C.B. stands as further indication of how far the bishops must still progress, intellectually and spiritually, if the forbidden fruit of collegiality is to be boldly distributed to the whole People of God. Both the hope and the embarrassment help to illuminate the shadows dappling the terrain under Vatican II's tree of knowledge, in the shade of which the "New Experiment in Democracy" will be conducted.

The "Call to Action" process, in itself, was a massive experiment in participatory democracy, unprecedented in the history of American Catholicism. Under the Bicentennial program of "Liberty and Justice for All," the American bishops, led by Cardinal John Dearden of Detroit, committed themselves to a three-stage consultation with American Catholics, beginning in 1975 with parish-level discussions and regional open hearings on problems of justice, to be followed by the national "Call to Action" conference in October 1976, whose recommendations were to be taken up by the National Conference of Catholic Bishops at their annual meeting in May 1977, and implemented, tested, and evaluated during the subsequent five-year period. The "Call to Action" process was a breakthrough, for it indissolubly wed traditional Catholic social teaching, heretofore concerned with substantive issues of justice in society as a whole, with the spirit of collegiality emanating from Vatican II, especially its concern for procedural justice within the church. Shared responsibility and due process, in other words, came to be seen as the indispensable precondition for pursuing justice, both inside and outside the church.

American Catholic response to the "Call to Action" process was strong. Throughout the United States, over 800,000 individual responses at the parish level contributed to shaping the working papers for the conference. While they certainly cannot be regarded as a statistically unbiased sample, the responses are a fairly good indication of the thinking of Catholics active and concerned enough to participate. At the conference itself, 1,340 delegates attended, representing 152 of the 167 Catholic dioceses and 92 national Catholic organizations. Although — or perhaps, precisely because — 93 percent of the delegates were appointed by bishops, blacks and other ethnic minorities within the church were unusually well represented. It is not insignificant that 39 percent of the delegates were women.[6] On the basis of their own special interest or expertise, the delegates divided themselves into eight section committees, each devoted to a specific theme in Catholic social teaching: the church, ethnicity and race, the family, humankind, nationhood, neighborhood, personhood, and work.[7] These in turn were subdivided into several working groups who were to formulate specific recommendations which, once they were collated and revised by the section committees, were to be taken back to the conference as a whole for a final vote. According to the Quixote Center's analysis of the "Call to Action," the real breakthrough occurred when "these small groups began to exercise independent judgment."[8]

The recommendations actually passed at the final plenary session themselves anticipate much of the agenda for the church's "New Experiment in Democracy." Throughout all of them runs a single theme, the suffering hope of activist Catholics that the whole "People of God," ordinary parish priests, professional religious, and all the diverse tribes of laity, be allowed to taste the forbidden fruit of collegiality. Under each of the eight themes, it is the notion of shared responsibility that brings the conference's recommendations into coherent focus. Conscious of their extraordinary diversity, the delegates called for the creation of an American Catholic church in which authority is shared on the basis of actual participation in the work of the community. Only such broadened participation would ensure that the value of diversity, so often extolled for American society as a whole, is also respected in the institutions of the church.

Here are the most noteworthy of the recommendations, divided according to the eight areas of Catholic social teaching:

● In their deliberations on justice in the church, the delegates called for collective bargaining for church employees, standardization of due process procedures nationwide, financial accountability for Catholic institutions, local participation in the selection of bishops, elimination of sexist language in church documents, and the ordination of women.

● Reflection on problems of ethnicity and race emphasized the church's failure to live up to its own teachings on "racial and ethnic equality" and advocated church support for affirmative action and the appointment of more ethnic, black, and Hispanic bishops.

● Their perspectives on family life expressed hope for a more pastoral approach to the problems of divorced and remarried Catholics than that embodied in the canonical penalty of automatic excommunication. They also asked for assistance in creating structures that would allow families to participate as families in the work of Catholic social action.

● Under the heading of personhood, besides reaffirming their general support for the bishops' pro-life ethic, the delegates championed the rights of individual conscience on moral questions involving birth control, called for more sensitive pastoral care for "sexual minorities" and victims of rape, and asked that the role of preacher be opened to women, young persons, and unordained men.[9]

In these four areas, then, "Liberty and Justice for All" became a cry for a new commitment to processes of collegiality. Women and minorities, professional religious, secular employees and ordinary laypersons are to share responsibility with priests and bishops at every level of authority within the church. In the following four areas, the focus shifts to problems affecting society as a whole.

● Concerning work, the delegates advocated establishment of a national commission on economic justice, ratification of the Equal Rights Amendment, and repeal of any legislation impeding the rights of workers to associate in labor unions. They defined the church's specific contribution in this area as, among other things, developing diocesan plans for equal opportunity employment and using church investments to lobby business corporations to work for social justice in the Third World.

● Under the category of neighborhood, their recommendations generally tended to see the church as having a role in the creation and support of local community organizations. Pastors of parishes should seek to form ecumenical networks and "outreach" coalitions interested in preserving and improving neighborhoods as human communities.

● Reflection on American nationhood brought out the delegates' support for both the bishops' pro-life program and the Equal Rights Amendment. But in addition to these ongoing activities, they also advocated initiating a "national commitment to a policy of peace and to programs of disarmament." Mindful of the "Call to Action" conference's unique status as a national assembly of American Catholics, the delegates asked the bishops to appoint a task force drawn from the delegates, charged with promoting "the implementation of all the conference's recommendations."

● Finally, turning their attention to the fate of "humankind," they condemned "the production, possession, proliferation and threatened use of nuclear weapons and all other weapons of indiscriminate effect, even in a policy of deterrence." The church could make a more effective contribution to serving humanity were it to establish "a network of diocesan justice and peace commissions" coordinating their efforts with the ongoing work of the U.S.C.C.[10]

While the results of the "Call to Action" conference thus anticipate some of the major issues featured in discussion of the current pastoral letters, what I must emphasize here is not the substantive "prophetic" content of its recommendations but the collegially democratic process by which they were formed. "Call to Action" was not a coup engineered by a tiny minority of professional activists intent on usurping the public agenda of the church in this country. On the contrary, a committee of the American bishops consulted the faithful in a process so open and expansive that it could not be manipulated by any particular interest group, including the bishops themselves. But the dynamics of the process, especially as it reached a climax at Detroit, stimulated an expansion of consciousness that could not help but judge the church's own practices by the same standard as they were being encouraged to use to judge other institutions in society: "Liberty and Justice for All."[11] Little wonder, then, that in the consensus emerging among the delegates, the credibility of the church's critical participation in the affairs of the world inescapably depends upon the quality of critical participation allowed in the church itself. The delegates had tasted the fruit of collegiality and their eyes were now open.

Some who found this new experience disturbing tried to discredit the "Call to Action" process, and its results, as "irresponsibly radical." The objections were partly substantive, partly procedural. We take them up here because they help illuminate some of the problems that will arise with the church's "New Experiment in Democracy." Procedural criticism centered, first, on the unrepresentative character of the conference participants and therefore the allegedly unrepresentative character of the opinions expressed there; the "Call to Action" process, in other words, had been coopted by "special interest groups." Other critics focused on the fact that the conference "tried to do too much and did it superficially"; the conference's schedule was so tight and the time to discuss each issue so limited, that any consensus reached that way would have to be dismissed as ill-considered and therefore incompetent. As the Quixote Center's analysis suggests, both of these procedural criticisms identify problems common to any truly open democratic process.

Let us consider first the alleged problem of special interest groups. At the time of the conference, this charge could only be deflected by conceding that the process was never meant to yield a sociological portrait of American Catholic opinion. Though studies done since then suggest that most of the recommendations enjoy significant support from ordinary Catholics,[12] it is possible to address this charge at the level of principle. For the problem of special interest groups is as old as the original American experiment in democracy. In *The Federalist Papers*, James Madison referred to them as "factions," and fully aware of the threat they posed, he reasoned that, since they were inherent in the associational nature of human beings, they could not be suppressed, at least not in a democracy. He proposed not the forced elimination of factions but rather, the opposite: "Extend the sphere [of a republic] and you take in a greater variety of parties and interests; you make it less probable that a majority of the whole will have a common motive to invade the rights of other citizens."[13]

Madison's insight, which lies at the foundation of this nation's federal system of government, also seems to have been in the minds of those who designed the "Call to Action" process. For rather than suppressing factions within the church, "Call to Action" tried to take advantage of their energy and commitment by encouraging them to focus upon their "special interests," but in a deliberative process large and diverse enough to ensure that no one group could succeed in dominating all the others. So the conference, rather unexpectedly, ended up achieving a consensus based not on the dominance of "special interests," but on the mutual recognition of persons who could reason together because each was especially interested. Of course, while faith alone can discern whether such group dynamics are the work of the Holy Spirit, it must be conceded that Madison's solution, though it works so well, yields necessarily tentative results. The validity of the consensus reached will always depend on the openness of the deliberative process itself.

Let us postpone consideration of the question of competence, and turn instead to substantive issues. Two areas in particular drew the wrath of critics bent on driving a wedge between "Call to Action" and the American bishops, the conference's recommendations regarding justice in the church and for humanity as a whole. It is not surprising that critics should regard as irresponsible calls for the ordination of women, optional celibacy for priests of either sex, and a reconsideration of Catholic teaching on birth control. For in these areas, the conference clearly was reopening issues that had been declared closed, even during the reign of Pope Paul VI. But it is surprising that the conference's recommendations calling for a reassessment of the United States' role in promoting social justice in the global economy, and denouncing American involvement with nuclear weapons, should receive the same kind of criticism. For in these areas "Call to Action" was merely developing papal teaching in the American context. The problem, then as now, was how to keep both sets of issues on the church's agenda since, as the conference in Detroit came to realize, both clearly stem from the church's sense of "Liberty and Justice for All." Under the circumstances, with discussion of the one set of topics repressed, and only the other currently acceptable for "open discussion" within the church, how could "Call to Action" not appear irresponsibly radical in insisting upon the seamless connection between the two?

"Call to Action's" critics were most impressively answered by Cardinal John Dearden in his "Report to the N.C.C.B.," issued within a week of the conference. In words reminiscent of Isaac Hecker, he noted that, "in general, the actions recommended to us indicate a realism, an independence, and a critical and mature judgment remarkable in a first assembly conducted along democratic lines."[14] Here is Cardinal Dearden's plea to his fellow bishops:

> The results of the bicentennial process may at this point seem hasty, untidy, careless, even extreme. But on closer examination, it seems to me that far more often the working papers and conference resolutions demonstrate a warmth and sympathy for the problems of Church leadership on the part of our people, their enthusiastic affirmation of Christian faith and hope, their sincere willingness to share in building a stronger Church, and their firm resolve to fulfill a Christian ministry to the world. No one expects us to

endorse all that transpired at Detroit. People do expect us to continue the process by responding with decisive action where it is called for, and with honest disagreement where that seems necessary. The key to our actions in the future is to continue the process, to build on the hopes that have been awakened, to act upon our clear responsibility for the unity, fidelity and vision of the Catholic community.

No less hopeful a sign than the conference itself, in light of the controversy it was generating, is Cardinal Dearden's willingness to defend it. For his words express that essentially Americanist trust that ordinary Catholics, when given the chance to exercise a "certain liberty" in church, will think and act responsibly.

Between the conference in Detroit and the American bishops' annual meeting the following May, Archbishop Joseph Bernadin, then President of the U.S.C.C./N.C.C.B., tried to defuse the "Call to Action" controversy but succeeded only in creating the impression that some American bishops want the forbidden fruit of collegiality to remain forbidden to all, except themselves. In appointing a task force for reviewing and implementing the conference's recommendations, Bernadin set aside the delegates' request that conference participants be named to the committee and appointed a task force composed mostly of bishops known to be critical of the conference. Significantly, the task force did not include either Cardinal Dearden or Archbishop Peter Gerety of Newark, who also had supported "Call to Action" enthusiastically. When the task force appeared poised to react negatively to the conference's recommendations, according to *The National Catholic Reporter*, Dearden had to intervene personally in order to save the process and its anticipated five-year schedule for implementation. Meanwhile, despite Bernadin's denial of engaging in any "delaying tactic(s)," the task force's actions and the secrecy surrounding its deliberations did nothing to relieve the perplexity of those who in good faith had participated in the "Call to Action" process.[15]

Rick Casey's column in *The National Catholic Reporter*, published the week of the bishops' annual meeting, testifies to the passion aroused by Archbishop Bernadin's actions:

> So while "A Call to Action" may have been one of the most ambitious democratic enterprises in the history of the American church, Bernadin's responsibility is not to those thousands who worked hard to put it together, nor even to those millions who did not participate, but to those few dozen in Rome whose idea of participatory democracy is allowing non-Italians in the College of Cardinals . . . . By selecting such a committee, Bernadin has done his best to bury the results of the Detroit conference.[16]

Though Casey may have been hasty in his characterization of Archbishop Bernadin's intentions, his insight into the principle at stake, namely, the scope of participatory democracy in the church, still seems valid. The archbishop's half-hearted attempt to dissociate the N.C.C.B. from the results that "Call to Action" produced, indicates an ambivalence about new experiments in democracy that still may linger in the minds of even "progressive" American bishops. How much longer will they, like Agamemnon at Aulis, continue to sacrifice their own spiritual progeny in order to placate the dead wind of counterrevolution from Rome? How much longer can they avoid facing the full implications of Vatican II's call for collegiality?

The eventual fruitfulness of the "Call to Action" process, obviously, remains to be seen. But even in its early stages the process had helped rekindle an already smouldering controversy over the nature of Catholic social action, when in 1975 the N.C.C.B.'s Committee for the Bicentennial issued its discussion guide for parishes and neighborhood organizations. This pamphlet, *Liberty and Justice for All*, was designed to stimulate initial response to the process at the grassroots level. It consisted of "resource papers" by prominent Catholic thinkers for each of the eight problem areas, accompanied by suggested policy questions that might be raised in preparation for the "Call to Action" conference. Piqued by the questions proposed, and by the content of some of the resource papers, Andrew Greeley denounced *Liberty and Justice for All* as the typical product of a new and problematic style of Catholic social action.

For all its rhetorical excess, Greeley's essay, "Catholic Social Activism — Real or Rad/Chic?," raises methodological issues regarding free and open discussion within the church that go to the heart of the problem of recreating an Americanist spirit in the church after Vatican II. Greeley opens up the problem by contrasting two models of Catholic social action, the old and the new, and seeking to go beyond both to something that is both older and newer than either. He summarizes the contrast between the old and the new, somewhat misleadingly, as "the differences between a pre-Berrigan and a post-Berrigan approach to influencing people and facilitating social change."[17] Appropriate slogans are used to model the contrast: competence versus concern; coalition-building versus confrontation. Fully aware of the risk of caricature involved in polarizing these differences, Greeley hoped to spark "a great debate" about an appropriately American style for activist Catholics.

The old style of Catholic social action, based on a group portrait of Greeley's heroes, priests in the tradition of John A. Ryan, George G. Higgins, Geno Baroni, and Jack Egan, is American pragmatism in a Roman collar. Such priests were — and still are — practical and project-oriented, tolerant of imperfection and willing to compromise, both good listeners and impressive doers. Self-consciously Catholic, these clerical power-brokers had — and still have — a knack for getting things done the American way. They instinctively promote Catholic ideals of social justice along lines set comfortably within the mainstream of the American ethos. As Greeley himself rather grandly interprets it, their operative theology is rooted in a lively sense of the church's mission of reconciliation, a forthright attempt to redeem American society while confessing, in tones that resonate well with Reinhold Niebuhr's Protestant Christian Realism, the universality of sin but not the equality of all sinners in guilt.[18] Reconciliation is no cheap grace, but a religious praxis that cultivates the difficult art of living faithfully in sin by skillful compromise and continual coalition-building. The legacy of this Catholic social activism in the old style thus is best epitomized for Greeley by his heroes' unpretentious competence and their tough-minded appreciation for the human condition.

Greeley's portrait of the new style, however, is anything but generous. In an *ad hominem* attack upon Peter Henriot and his associates at the Jesuit Center of Concern, Catholic "rad/chic" is characterized as obsessed with the will-o'-the-wisp of systemic social analysis, doctrinaire and ideological in its approach to politics, and morally perfectionist in its theology. The new style, according to Greeley, succeeds only in being simultaneously anti-American and marginally Catholic. For it is captive to "the evil genius" of Paulo Freire, the Brazilian educator whose theory of consciousness-raising helped stimulate the formulation of Latin American liberation theology.[19] In Greeley's view, the resulting approach to Catholic social action exhausts itself in issuing arrogant and ill-informed manifestoes, and in laying guilt trips on Catholics already involved in the struggle for justice. Unlike some of his heroes, Greeley contends that free and open dialogue is impossible on terms set by the new style of Catholic social activism.

Whatever the accuracy and fairness of these contrasting models, Greeley uses them first to air his own grievances against the discussion guide, *Liberty and Justice for All*. Though there are a few essays representative of the old style, in Greeley's view the discussion guide as a whole is dominated by the new. In particular he focuses his ire on an essay co-authored by Henriot and Jorge Dominguez, on "Humankind;" on Jesus Garcia Gonzalez's "The Church in the United States: A Latin American View;" and on the "Discussion Series" policy questions formulated by Dale Olen and Sister Francis Borgia Rothleubber. Henriot and Dominguez's attempt to characterize the problems of "our global community today" is dismissed as being "quite innocent of any sophisticated knowledge" of international economics. Gonzalez's uncomprehending disdain for American Catholic suburban and inner-city parish life is cited as evidence of his incompetence as a sociologist. And Olen and Rothleubber's simple-minded questions about Watergate and America's ability to celebrate the meaning of the Bicentennial suggest the discussion guide's adherence to the pedagogical method of Paulo Freire. Putting it all together, Greeley condemns the booklet as the work of "a small, uninformed elite," themselves the accomplices of "the liberal wing of the American hierarchy," who have turned from "support for Vietnam to America-hating . . . with astonishing speed."[20]

Greeley tries to back up these denunciations by offering four grounds for rejecting the discussion guide. He charges it with being (1) "unscholarly, simplistic, doctrinaire," (2) "historically false," (3) "disastrous psychologically," and (4) "hypocritical." Once they have been detached from Greeley's polemic, these charges ought to be given serious consideration. For, however irrelevant they may be in judging *Liberty and Justice for All*, each raises a question concerning the kinds of competence that must be integrated if the church's "New Experiment in Democracy" is to succeed. The first two charges, of course, raise the issue of professional competence: on public policy questions, is an objective assessment of the circumstances to which the religious community is responding either possible or desirable? The third charge, in my view, brings up the question of religious competence: what moral tone should be set and by whom in the religious community, when addressing public policy questions? Put in theological terms, the question of religious competence is a question, among other things, of the authenticity of self-consciously "prophetic" forms of Christian witness. The last charge, the accusation of hypocrisy, raises questions of communicative competence: since actions speak louder than words, what do consistency and good faith require of any community entering into public moral dialogue? While we will discuss in chapter four how these three forms of competence can be interrelated systematically, here it is important to note that Greeley's charges do call for critical reflection on problems that are endemic in Americanist Catholic religious praxis.

Let us, then, review Greeley's accusations in greater detail, for they do suggest how a "newer" form of Catholic activism might overcome the inadequacies of both the old and the new styles outlined in his contrasting models. Over and above his concern for bias in social analysis, Greeley emphasizes the disastrous consequences of "guilt-tripping" people in order to stir them into action for social justice, and the credibility problem created by continuing injustice within the church itself. While "guilt-tripping" is often counterproductive, the real danger involved in this psychological stratagem occurs when it is used to preempt the ordinary workings of a Madisonian "scheme of representation" and thus seize control of the community's public agenda. Though hardly applicable to the "Call to Action" process in any of its phases, Greeley's warnings usefully indicate how far the church has already progressed in its "New Experiment in Democracy." For only in such an experiment could any of his fears ever be realized.

So in defining a "newer" model of Catholic social activism, Greeley wants to avoid the various forms of incompetence that are distinctive of an expanded religious praxis of collegiality. On a more positive note, however, he proposes seven features for the "newer" model that in various ways build upon the achievements of both pre- and post-Berrigan activists. Though he does not explicitly make the connection, each of these appears to be in historic continuity with the Americanist spirit of Isaac Hecker and his followers. The seven may be reduced to certain dispositions of character desirable in all participants who would accept a share of responsibility for the church's social witness: (1) a humble acceptance of "the grayness and uncertainty of reality"; (2) a generosity of spirit that refuses to write off human nature as totally "depraved"; (3) a patient "hope . . . [for] . . . greater freedom and greater humanity" based on faith in the slowly maturing "dynamic of the resurrection" in history; (4) perseverance in the struggle for social justice, that is not shaken by the inevitable passing of one's own youthful enthusiasms; (5) diligence in acquiring "professional competence to deal intelligently and creatively with . . . [society's] . . . problems"; (6) a temperance that refuses to let one's Christian outrage at injustice become a pretext for "scapegoat[ing] others"; and (7) the evangelical courage to preach and practice a "reconciliation" that continually "rehumanizes the adversary."[21]

These seven dispositions, on the one hand, recall the four cardinal virtues, prudence, justice, fortitude, and temperance, celebrated by the ancient Roman moralists, and on the other hand, resonate well with the empiricist and pragmatic temper of the American people. But above all, Greeley's emerging model of Catholic social action stresses competence. Not that Catholic activists need become either secular technocrats or ecclesiastical careerists. Mere professionalization is not the point. Instead, Greeley seems to be recommending an integration of professional and religious competence, based on an underlying recognition of the exigencies of communicative competence, as I will argue in chapter four, among all those who participate in public dialogue. Were such competences to be fully integrated in the church's consultative processes, they might serve as a catalyst for "free and open discussion" about matters of public policy in society as a whole. His "newer" model of Catholic social activism thus takes us back to one of John Courtney Murray's deepest concerns.

Murray's Americanist vision of religious liberty, you will recall, emerges from the distinctively American experience of religious pluralism. Murray was properly ambivalent about the practical consequences of religious pluralism, for he realized that the obvious benefits of individual liberty of conscience must be weighed against the consideration that a lack of religious consensus might undermine our capacity to form a political community.[22] If there were no commonly accepted religious tradition, on what basis might the public argument that sustains us as a political nation be carried on? Rather than abandon American pluralism for the sake of a European-style nationalism, Murray dug more deeply into the American experience and discovered the pervasive but generally unrecognized tradition of "civility" that continually reconstitutes our one nation from the diverse peoples living here.

There is nothing particularly Christian about this civility; but neither is it exclusively secular. It is, as Murray said, "a thing of the surface. It is quite easy to break through it. And when you do, you catch a glimpse of the factual reality of the pluralist society."[23] Civility is, in short, a disposition to conduct politics not as open warfare among conflicting interest groups but as skillful and self-disciplined public "conversation."[24] For the opposite of civility is not political "conspiracy" as such, but "barbarism" in the pursuit of one's interests. In our pluralistic society, each major community of faith, "Protestant, Catholic, Jewish, secularist," helps sustain the political "conversation" by conspiring with others to keep their respective traditions of civility alive and in good working order. The result Murray envisions is modest, but significant:

> We cannot hope to make American society the perfect conspiracy based on a unanimous consensus. But we could at least do two things. We could limit the warfare, and we could enlarge the dialogue. We could lay down our arms (at least the more barbarous kind of arms!), and we could take up argument. [25]

Notwithstanding Greeley's characteristically uncivil way of presenting it, his "newer" model for social activism — especially its seven ideal character traits — must be taken seriously as an attempt to keep the Catholic tradition of civility from disappearing altogether.

With the hindsight afforded by an additional decade of turmoil within both the Catholic church and American society as a whole, it should be easier to see the real issues involved in

Greeley's projected "great debate" and their meaning for the church's "New American Experiment in Democracy." The virtues that he recommends to social activists both old and new merit our attention. For they give a coherent picture of what it will take for Catholics to hold up their end of the American civil "conversation." The four cardinal virtues of the ancient Roman moral tradition, coupled with a primitively American respect for "know-how" and common sense and nurtured by an authentically Catholic reverence for the redemptive possibilities in ordinary human nature: these are dispositions that must distinguish civility from barbarism in the church's approach to justice, not just in society but also in the church itself. For what Greeley has identified is not simply one more distinct theological "model" for Catholic social activism, but the boundary conditions governing any theological model building in a society premissed on the notion of "self-governing association."

Judged by Greeley's own model, however, the "Call to Action" process deserves a better verdict than the pamphlet used to get it rolling. The agenda was, as Cardinal Dearden reported, overly ambitious; and there certainly was conspiracy. But the conspiracy at Detroit was more like the one that Murray had hoped for than the one that Greeley feared. Though clearly not "a perfect conspiracy based on unanimous consensus," the "Call to Action" results did "enlarge the dialogue" within the church and prepared the ground for later "argument." Those who participated saw justice issues very well in the situations they knew best, that is, in the ordinary routines of the institutional church. By insisting, in effect, that the church must practice in its own routines what it preaches to the rest of society, they set a standard of communicative competence for religious communities engaged in public "conversation." Most importantly, their willingness to set aside competitive pressures and really learn from each other, to trust the professional and religious competence of those whose contributions lay behind the work of other committees, suggests a "civility" based on something deeper than the usual conventions of interest group politics. In short, at Detroit the "Call to Action" delegates helped create a religious praxis whose promise can and ought to be fulfilled in the church's "New Experiment in Democracy."

While the recent pastoral letters on war and peace and the U.S. economy are not part of the "Call to Action" process, they do, along with a proposed new pastoral letter on the role of women in the church, respond to central concerns raised in that process and carry further in new ways its experiment with Americanist forms of religious praxis. For if "Call to Action" in seeking to implement Catholic social teaching managed to raise fundamental questions about the nature of that teaching, the pastoral letters are seeking to answer these questions, both procedurally and substantively. Moreover the process involved in the drafting of these pastoral letters, in my view, would not have occurred, but for the bishops' ability to learn from "Call to Action" and the controversy surrounding it. The most obvious connection between "Call to Action" and the pastoral letter process is the unprecedented openness of the discussions involved in the drafting of the letters. The format of public hearings, in which bishops themselves listen to, and enter into public argument with, Catholics and others concerned about the principles and policy issues to be discussed in the letters, not only marks another new expansion in the praxis of collegiality, but also hearkens back to the Americanist tradition of Catholic civility celebrated by Murray. Out of these hearings has also come a way of making Greeley's concerns about competence within the church amenable to the test of experience. Though the consultations were designed to accomplish different objectives, "Call to Action" thus helped shape the pastoral letter process as a process, as well as the actual teaching and pedagogy emerging in the letters themselves.

So far the best documented illustration of the similarities and differences linking these two processes is the conference on "Catholic Social Teaching and the U.S. Economy," organized for the drafting committee in December 1983, by the Center for Ethics and Religious Values in Business at the University of

Notre Dame.[26] The very structure of the Notre Dame conference provided the bishops' committee with a new vehicle for testing the various types of competence involved in drafting a pastoral letter. The three levels of competence identified in the "Call to Action" controversy, communicative, professional, and religious, were all evident in the public hearing, but their focus was more narrowly centered on the role of competent professionals in helping the bishops to achieve clarity about their own teachings. For in contrast to "Call to Action," the Notre Dame conference was not a popular deliberative assembly designed to help discern the church's common agenda for social action. Instead, though it was open to the public, actual participation at the Notre Dame hearing was limited to professionals chosen to facilitate the formation of consensus among the bishops about the very meaning of Catholic social teaching. Future development in the church's practice of collegiality, including its "New American Experiment in Democracy," will depend on how consensus is formed, if at all, in consultation processes designed not just to implement Catholic social teaching but to determine its content in the first place.

Thus the Notre Dame conference featured a format structured differently from the "Call to Action" process. First of all, the hearings were organized not around certain basic themes of Catholic social teaching, but around specific policy questions where public opinion is divided, not only in the church, but in society as a whole. Second, the panelists for each hearing were chosen with two criteria in mind: first, at least one of them had to have professional competence in interpreting the traditions of Catholic social teaching so that each panel would include explicit discussion of the theological and ethical principles at stake in the policy controversies; second, the experts chosen to speak on the policy questions were expected to reflect the controversies so that the drafting committee would get a more detached view of the issues involved, and not just a plea advocating a particular policy or perspective. Third, at each hearing, after brief summaries by the panelists of the arguments laid out in their predistributed position papers, ample time was scheduled for open discussion involving not only the panelists, the members of the drafting committee, and their staff of advisers, but also any of the invited participant observers at the conference. Finally, at the end of the conference, the drafting committee held a press conference at which they fielded questions concerning what they hoped to accomplish with the pastoral letter and what they had learned from the experience. The Notre Dame conference, in short, was modeled less like a town meeting in colonial New England, and more like a congressional hearing on some piece of pending legislation.

Though hardly in the grassroots style of "Call to Action," the conference at Notre Dame did involve the bishops present in a learning process in which competence could be achieved and demonstrated in public. Its manifest commitment to "free and open discussion" was restricted only by the limits of those invited to participate. The two hundred and fifty participants were sufficiently diverse in their opinions, but no doubt they were selected on the basis of their achievements. The inarticulate poor, however, may have been better represented at some of the other meetings that more closely resembled the "Call to Action" hearings. Nevertheless, this possible slippage away from the ideal of communicative competence was accompanied by a corresponding gain in professional competence. Though many of the participants, including the members of the drafting committee, made statements criticizing various aspects of the U.S. economy, none of them could be accused of being either ignorant or contemptuous of the workings of American institutions. Presumably, by the end of the learning process, the bishops will be able to demonstrate a competence in matters of economic policy at least equal to that of our elected representatives in Washington.

The most striking similarity between the Notre Dame conference and "Call to Action" lies in the participating bishops' approach to religious competence, their own and that of their conversation partners. My own experience at Notre Dame echoes the Quixote Center's account of what transpired at Detroit. Though in no way abdicating their own role, the bishops disarmingly refused to hide behind their own authority. They seemed eager to enter fully and unguardedly into the work of the conference. Hardly self-conscious in doing so, they generally conducted themselves in that refreshingly straightforward style that Hecker, Ireland, and Elliott had once envisioned for an authentically American Catholic clergy. In conversation with various panelists and participants, they acted more as facilitators of an open-ended process seeking fresh consensus, rather than as presiders over a sterile debate whose outcome had already been decided elsewhere. Even in the area of religious competence, they seemed bent on earning their own way.

As I write these words, the pastoral letter process has yet to run its course. For now it stands as a hopeful sign that American Catholicism has yet to repent of eating the forbidden fruit of collegiality. The "Call to Action" process, precisely because of the controversy surrounding it, made us acutely aware of the knowledge of good and evil that is the promise of Vatican II. It rekindled our desire to share the fruit of collegiality by demonstrating once more that ordinary American Catholics, as well as their bishops, are capable of exercising that "certain liberty" in church, not just to the benefit of the church but also in service to society as a whole. Alongside the irrepressible "Americanist heresy," remembering "Call to Action" can become a sign of what the practice of collegiality could still bring were the tree of knowledge allowed to flourish in an atmosphere conducive to participatory democracy. This unashamedly partisan recollection of "Call to Action" thus makes our remembering the Americanist heresy still more dangerous: while we still lack a theology capable of grounding a "New Experiment in Democracy" in our own traditions, our eyes are now open to the diverse demands of competence in any authentically American Catholic religious praxis.

Notes

1. *Dogmatic Constitution on the Church (Lumen Gentium)*, par. 22, in Walter M. Abbott, ed., *The Documents of Vatican II* (London: Geoffrey Chapman, 1967), p. 43.

2. Cf. Robert Blair Kaiser, *The Politics of Sex and Religion* (Kansas City, Missouri: Leaven Press, 1985), pp. 59-67.

3. *Decree on the Bishops' Pastoral Office in the Church (Christus Dominus)*, par. 38, in Walter M. Abbott, ed., *op. cit.*, p. 425.

4. *Constitution on the Sacred Liturgy (Sacrosanctum Concilium)*, par. 22, *ibid.*, p. 146.

5. James Hennesey S.J., *American Catholics: A History of the Roman Catholic Community in the United States* (New York: Oxford University Press, 1981) p. 315.

6. Quixote Center Staff, "What Happened at Detroit? Were We Mugged or Blessed?" (Hyattsville, Maryland: Quixote Center, 1977), p. 3.

7. Catholic Committee on Urban Ministry, Philip J. Murnion, Chairman, *Handbook: A Call to Action* (Notre Dame, Indiana: Catholic Committee on Urban Ministry, 1976), p. 1.

8. Quixote Center Staff, *art. cit.*, p. 3.

9. "Delegates call for action in eight subject areas," in the *National Catholic Reporter* (5 November 1976), p. 16. Cf. Quixote Center Staff, *art. cit.*, p. 5-11, 17-8.

10. "Ibid.," in the *National Catholic Reporter*; Cf. Quixote Center Staff, *art. cit.*, p. 11-6, 18-20.

11. Quixote Center Staff, *art. cit.*, p. 5.

12. Cf. Andrew Greeley, *American Catholics: A Social Portrait* (New York: Basic Books, 1977); cf. Andrew Greeley, *American Catholics Since the Council: An Unauthorized Report* (Chicago: Thomas More Press, 1985); cf. David C. Leege and Joseph Gremillion, "The People, Their Pastors, and the Church: Viewpoints on Church Policies and Positions," Report No. 7 in Leege and Gremillion, eds., *Notre Dame Study of Catholic Parish Life* (Notre Dame, Indiana: Institute for Pastoral and Social Ministry and the Center for the Study of Contemporary Society, University of Notre Dame, March, 1986).

13. James Madison, "Federalist Paper No. 10," in Clinton Rossiter, ed., *The Federalist Papers* (New York: New American Library, 1961), pp. 77-84.

14. Cardinal John Dearden, "Report on the Justice Conference, November 9, 1976," in Catholic Committee on Urban Ministry, *op. cit.*, p. 3.

15. Mark Winiarski, "Cardinal fights to save 'Call to Action' process," in the *National Catholic Reporter* (April 22, 1977), p. 1, 31.

16. Rick Casey, "Bernadin as boss," in the *National Catholic Reporter* (May 6, 1977), p. 2.

17. Andrew Greeley, "Catholic social activism — real or rad/chic?," in the *National Catholic Reporter* (February 7, 1975), pp. 7-11.

18. Cf. Reinhold Niebuhr, *The Nature and Destiny of Man, Vol.I* (New York: Charles Scribner's Sons, 1964), pp. 219-227. For an interpretation of Christian Realism, see Dennis P. McCann, *Christian Realism and Liberation Theology: Practical Theologies in Creative Conflict* (Maryknoll, New York: Orbis Books, 1981), pp. 6-130.

19. For an interpretation of the work of Paulo Freire in relation to the methodology of liberation theology, see McCann, *op. cit.*, pp. 156-175.

20. Greeley, *art. cit.*, p. 8.

21. *Ibid.*, p. 10-11.

22. John Courtney Murray, *We Hold These Truths: Catholic Reflections on the American Proposition* (Garden City, New York: Doubleday Image Books, 1964), pp. 17-35.

23. *Ibid.*, p. 30.

24. *Ibid.*, p. 25.

25. *Ibid.*, p. 34.

26. Cf. John W. Houck and Oliver F. Williams, eds., *Catholic Social Teaching and the U.S. Economy: Working Papers for a Bishops' Pastoral* (Washington, D.C.: University Press of America, 1984).

3

SELECTIVE CATHOLICISM: LIVING OUT THE DEATH OF THE IMMIGRANT CHURCH

I feel we should resist the facile solution that the bishops are theoreticians and lay people empiricists. Vatican II does see the field of the laity as that of concrete involvement, but it also sees the bishops reflecting on the whole — not just the part. So I find this division artificial and unreal. On the other hand, I am just as unhappy that bishops seem to be monopolizing the moral debate on these issues. Perhaps the process used . . . [in drafting the pastoral letters] . . . helps avoid that false dichotomy.

— Archbishop Rembert G. Weakland, Woodstock Forum on the Bishops' Pastoral, *Woodstock Report*, May, 1985.

Over three quarters of a century separates "Call to Action" and the recent pastoral letter process from the condemnation of the Americanist heresy. During the intervening years of spiritual exile and cultural isolation, American Catholics for the most part lived in a ghetto now known to historians as "the immigrant church." This style of Catholic religious praxis, characterized by "integralism" in theology and "devotionalism" in spirituality, accentuated the differences separating American Catholics from their fellow citizens: unquestioning loyalty to Rome, a veneration of the Blessed Virgin and the saints that at least bordered on the superstitious, clerical authoritarianism, and a consciousness of sin that made all these other differences seem not just plausible but indispensable. It was an ecclesiastical style that left ordinary Catholics with little alternative but, in the words of historian Jay Dolan, to "pay, pray, and obey."[1]

It will not come as news to hear that the immigrant church is dead. What passed away, of course, was not exclusively a church of immigrants. For the self-imposed ghetto that we're remembering emerged during the 1920s after the major waves of immigration once the earlier Americanist tradition had been aborted by the Vatican. Largely the creation of the autocratic Romanizing bishops who succeeded Cardinal Gibbons' generation, not without success it represented a defensive, or if you will, militant way of life that was, in the words of Eugene Kennedy, "tight, intellectually narrow, and wrapped in an invisible and largely impermeable membrane that resisted social osmosis with the rest of the country."[2] This way of life died of sclerosis, when the membrane ceased having a plausible function.

While, within the shelter of this Catholic ghetto, millions of immigrant families endured their rite of passage toward "naturalized" American citizenship, already before its dismantling at Vatican II their children were catching up with Protestants in economic and educational achievement. What killed the immigrant church was the massive entry of Catholics into the mainstream of the American middle class.[3] The more successful American Catholics became, the more dysfunctional also became that "invisible and largely impermeable membrane." Not that the immigrant experience doesn't continue to make Catholics different in significant ways from other middle class Americans, but no longer must they see themselves in terms of the images hallowed by "devotional Catholicism." Ordinary Catholics aren't "sheep" anymore who must blindly obey "shepherds" in order to insure their social survival.

Death brings with it a number of intense, but conflicting, emotions; it also opens up new challenges and opportunities for those who must go on living. Bereavement thus is sometimes accompanied by a sense of relief, but just as often by feelings of abandonment, with their inevitable accompaniment of rage, confusion, and guilt. This is no less true when an institution dies: as the institution is interred and, sometimes, reborn, there is a critical period of transition in which these emotions are played out, with both creative and destructive consequences for the possibilities that lie ahead. For American Catholicism the period after Vatican II has been, among other things, such a time of bereavement.[4] Those who grew up in that "tight, intellectually narrow" subculture are embracing the new possibilities opened up by the death of the immigrant church, but they are doing so with all the emotional conflict usually associated with a death in the family.

Vatican II did not cause the death of the immigrant church, but its passing did coincide with the Council's universal call for church reform or *aggiornamento*. Much of the feeling inspired by this death has thus been transferred to Vatican II. The sense of relief, as well as the rage, confusion, and guilt have all been so intensely focused on the meaning of Vatican II that they seem to be obscuring the new possibility that lies beyond the death of the immigrant church. Instead of laboring for the rebirth of an authentically American Catholicism, Catholics are tending to become polarized in various forms of what Andrew Greeley has called "selective Catholicism."[5] This polarization seems to be jeopardizing the church's capacity to learn much from either its long-term or its short-term dangerous memories. Those currently most vocal in reasserting the Americanist tradition seem bent on repudiating attempts, like "Call to Action," to democratize the church; those most zealous for expanding collegiality to include the whole People of God seem curiously unaware of their roots in the Americanist tradition. The church's "New American Experiment in Democracy" cannot help but fail, unless this polarization can be overcome. But in order to overcome it, we must first understand "selective Catholicism," its pervasiveness today, and its ambiguous relationship to an authentically American Catholicism.

The emergence of "selective Catholicism" is a major theme in Andrew Greeley's most recent sociological study, *American Catholics Since the Council: An Unauthorized Report*.[6] The trends that he previously analyzed in *The American Catholic: A Social Portrait* generally seem to be intensifying, but with some important new wrinkles. Over the past ten years the educational and economic achievements of Catholics in this country have clearly surpassed those of Protestants, while Catholic political opinion has remained slightly left of center. The decline in church attendance that was supposed to have signalled, at long last, a secularizing trend among Catholics, cannot be attributed to the alleged confusion generated by the reforms of Vatican II, but seems to be a brief episode explainable specifically as the result of a "single jolt," Pope Paul VI's encyclical, *Humanae vitae* (1968), condemning "artificial" means of birth control. While the vast majority of American Catholics dissent from the teachings of that encyclical, they have not left the church. Correlating this somewhat surprising finding with other indicators, Greeley argues that perhaps "four-fifths of the regular Sunday church attenders"[7] have begun to live a kind of "selective Catholicism" in which, while remaining "loyal" to the church, they ignore official church teaching in those areas where they judge papal and episcopal leadership to be incompetent.

The forces creating this American style of "selective Catholicism" are complex. The changes in Catholic doctrine, worship, and church discipline implemented in the wake of Vatican II provided a suitable atmosphere, as did the rise of an "educated and independent" laity capable of living with the ambiguity of change. The controversy over birth control, however, was the specific flash point: for, as Robert Blair Kaiser has recently documented, the protracted debate during the Council, the massive publicity given to the conflicting moral perspectives of the papal birth control commission, and press reports that the majority of the commission members actually favored a change in church teaching, encouraged ordinary Catholics to follow their own opinions in this area.[8] When *Humanae vitae* rejected the recommendation of the majority and, instead, reasserted the church's traditional prohibition on birth control, these same Catholics were consoled and encouraged by many theologians and pastors who helped them to understand that it was possible to remain loyal to the church while following the church's teachings on a selective basis.

As Greeley sees it, this new style of religious loyalty correlates positively with an increasingly prominent shift in the religious imagination of ordinary Catholics, away from images and stories of God as the dispenser of just punishments and toward images and stories that envision God as a warm and loving spouse or parent.[9] Fortified by personal assurance of a loving God, Catholics are emerging from their experience of church dissent "paradoxically" strengthened in their faith and loyalty to the Catholic tradition. The paradox is resolved, however, by redefining the nature of religious loyalty. After the death of the immigrant church, ordinary Catholics are becoming as comfortably familiar with church as they previously became with their ethnic group membership and their political party affiliation. Parallel to their tendency to insist upon personal independence even as they remain "loyal" to these increasingly voluntary associations, such people are remaining Catholic on a "do-it-yourself" basis. As in these other areas, they are setting the terms of their own commitment, and they are convinced that God cannot possibly be angry with them for doing so.

The most striking evidence of the positive side of this "selective Catholicism" is available in survey data on lay Catholic response to the bishops' 1983 pastoral letter on nuclear weapons. Greeley expected to find a carry-over effect, according to which ordinary Catholics would have ignored the pastoral letter because of their negative attitudes toward church teaching on sexual ethics. If the bishops are wrong in one area of Catholic social teaching, they must be wrong in all areas. Instead, much to his surprise, Greeley found that the letter had produced a measurable positive impact on Catholic opinion. Whereas in early 1983, before the letter was released, 34 percent of Catholics surveyed joined the same percentage of Protestants in thinking that too much money was being spent on national defense; a year later, after the letter's release, while the Protestant figure remained at 34 percent, the percentage of Catholics subscribing to that opinion shot up to 54 percent. As Greeley himself comments:

> Devoid of credibility in sexual ethics, the American hierarchy turns out to have enormous credibility on matters of nuclear policy, probably more credibility than they themselves thought they possessed and certainly more than most outside observers would have anticipated. In fact, it may well be said that the effective leadership of the American bishops on the nuclear weapons question represents a power and an influence of leadership which does not seem to be matched anywhere in the world.[10]

Although some of this increase in opposition to excessive defense spending represents a return to earlier views among lay Catholics, still there is a dramatic shift of some fifteen percentage points that cannot be explained away.[11] The reception of the pastoral letter suggests that the loyalty involved in "selective Catholicism" is real: the do-it-yourself attitude is balanced by, among other things, a moral seriousness that is willing to listen to the bishops when their teachings make sense. Popular response to the pastoral letter is obviously not just a reaction to the bishops' preaching what the laity want to hear. For before the letter was issued, Catholic opinion displayed a profile no different from Protestant opinion. Minds were changed, in my view, because the pastoral letter process allowed the bishops to address the laity as mature American adults.

As Greeley notes, however, most of the effective teaching of the letter occurred not under the auspices of the church but through the nation's news media.[12] The news coverage, which made vivid the process of debating the various drafts of the letter, allowed the bishops to appear before the nation as moral

teachers who, ostensibly, had done their homework. Furthermore, much to the dismay of those who opposed it, the letter
emerged at "a teachable moment." Here is Greeley's description
of it:

> In the year 1983 with the spread of the nuclear freeze
> movement and a general growing concern about the
> nuclear arms race in the United States and indeed in
> the rest of the world, there seems to have been a con-
> siderable unease among a segment of the American
> population, particularly those who for one reason or
> another were ill at ease with President Reagan and
> his defense policy. It would appear that the American
> bishops provided Catholics with this orientation with
> a focus for their concern which was not provided by
> any parallel agency or institution for American Pro-
> testants.[13]

So, in a sense, the bishops' success as moral teachers was really
due to circumstances beyond their control. But that in no way
detracts from the sincerity and integrity of those do-it-yourself
Catholics whose loyalty to the church was strong enough to
allow their teachers a serious hearing.

"Selective Catholicism" thus turns out to be something
more than an expediency born of what its critics have called the
"'contraceptive' mentality."[14] Though Greeley repeatedly insists that, as a sociologist, he can merely report on the phenomenon and not judge it theologically, an essay in practical theology is bound to scrutinize this new style of religious loyalty for
its authenticity. How one judges "selective Catholicism" will depend on how one interprets Catholic tradition. My own view, of
course, is premised on an intentionally dangerous reading of
American Catholic history, a reading that identifies what was
condemned as the Americanist heresy as the key to our past and
therefore our present and future. Seen in this light, "selective
Catholicism" is Americanist to the extent that, like Hecker, it

boldly affirms the presence of the Holy Spirit in the experiences of ordinary believers. It is also what an Americanist might expect, were Murray's rejection of "integralism" to penetrate to the grassroots level. Do-it-yourself Catholicism thus may be welcomed as the activity of the Holy Spirit seeking through dissent to creat a new *sensus fidelium*, the divinely inspired "consensus of the faithful" which forms the essence of the church at any given moment in its history.

Before we wholeheartedly accept this view, we must remember, as Hecker insisted, that the presence of the Holy Spirit is no less active in the authoritative structures of the church. When the two are in apparent conflict, open and honest dialogue between them is called for. Nothing essential to the practice of this new kind of religious loyalty, however, amounts to a refusal of dialogue. Dissent from *Humanae vitae* and other church teachings, in the vast majority of cases, has been responsible and responsive. As Greeley pointed out, those dissenting did not leave the church, but tried to work out an accommodation with the help of sympathetic pastors. Were it not for its usually implicit recognition of the legitimate claims of church authority, "selective Catholicism" might rightly be dismissed as the brazen expression of "hedonism and materialism" in the church. Nevertheless, the challenge raised by "selective Catholicism" is not whether there is any legitimate authority in the church, but the manner of its legitimation in a church already well underway with various experiments in democracy.

Though I find myself in basic agreement with the liberal consensus reflected in the recommendations of the "Call to Action" conference, in scrutinizing "selective Catholicism," I cannot ignore the protests of a vocal and articulate group of conservative Catholics, who also have had a significant impact on the recent pastoral letters. This group includes both a remnant of the pre-Conciliar "integralist" tradition and those neoconservatives whose ideology resonates with certain aspects of the older Americanist agenda. As inheritors of the legacy of the Americanist heresy, just as much as the progressives active in

the "Call to Action" process, these neoconservatives have carried on a war of words against "selective Catholicism" and have
been in the forefront of criticism opposing certain aspects of the
bishops' pastoral letters and the process that stands behind
them. In analyzing their protest, I will show that their denunciations of "selective Catholicism," and especially their dissent
from the pastoral letters, amount to a zealous campaign for an
equally "selective" version of American Catholicism. My point in
making this argument is not to pronounce anathema on the
neoconservatives, but to suggest that they, just as much as the
liberals inspired by the "Call to Action" process, need to acknowledge their own selectivity so that they, too, can contribute
to the church's "New Experiment in Democracy."

One convenient measure of the way both groups are responding to the death of the immigrant church and the
emergence of a "selective Catholicism" is their conflicting reactions to the so-called "Extraordinary Synod" that Pope John
Paul II announced for the fall of 1985 to celebrate the twentieth
anniversary of Vatican II. It was also called to evaluate the
achievements of that Council, the prospect of which occasioned
no end of speculation, intensifying the polemics on both sides.
In contrast to liberal perspectives on the Synod, featured by
America in September, 1985,[15] the neoconservative symposium
published earlier in June by *Catholicism in Crisis*[16] tends to
blame a distorted and distorting "Spirit of Vatican II" for all
that's gone wrong in the church during the past two decades. Admittedly, most of these writers remain rather coy about the
teachings of Vatican II itself. Michael Novak and Robert Royal,
noting that the Council launched a number of "experiments" in
the church, ask the Extraordinary Synod simply to "test" these
and to terminate those that have failed. Ronald Lawler calls for
distinguishing the true Vatican II from "the false Vatican IIs,"
while Richard Roach denounces the movement of "pseudo-re-
form following the Second Vatican Council . . . [as] . . . a recrudescence of Pharisaism." Generally, the neoconservatives
seem to agree with Cardinal Joseph Ratzinger's negative view
of the post-Conciliar church,[17] and look to the Pope to correct

certain "errors" in interpreting the Council's decrees, unilaterally if necessary. The liberals, not surprisingly, were not impressed by Cardinal Ratzinger's assessment, and welcomed the Synod as an opportunity to challenge his view.

When they get beyond generalities about the need to straighten out "current disorders" afflicting the church, the neoconservatives tend to focus on certain key issues: birth control and sexual ethics, freedom of conscience and the presence of the Holy Spirit within the church, the nature and tasks of seminary education, and, of course, the role of national episcopal conferences in implementing the Council's doctrine of collegiality. Regarding the question of birth control, Richard Roach, for example, agrees with Andrew Greeley in seeing this controversy as the point of departure for current dissent within the church. But, unlike Greeley, he advocates reasserting *Humanae vitae* in order to begin "the restoration of sound teaching." Many of the contributors take special aim at freedom of conscience. Royal asks rhetorically, "Do the rights of conscience mean that obedience to superiors is unnecessary whenever 'mature, adult Christians with autonomous consciences who do not need permission from anyone' unilaterally decide so?" And Lawler reminds his readers that freedom of conscience implies a moral obligation to "form conscience in the light of insistent Catholic teaching." It would appear that these authors are reluctant to trust the experience of ordinary believers, whenever it departs from the canons of orthodoxy.

The drama occasioned by the passing of the immigrant church and the emergence of "selective Catholicism" is also played out over the question of seminary education. Jude Dougherty, for example, faults the N.C.C.B.'s "Interim Guidelines for Seminary Renewal" and "Program for Priestly Formation" for not upholding the privileged position that scholastic philosophy traditionally enjoyed in the education of priests. He complains that while instructions from the Vatican see philosophy as "an indispensable key to culture and spiritual heritage," the N.C.C.B. documents regard it as a "humanistic discipline alongside others which have equal value and which may be substituted for it."[18] The N.C.C.B. apparently is to be faulted for having embraced an idea of philosophy which is indigenous to the American philosophical tradition and responsive to the logic of a pluralistic society. What is at stake here, however, may not simply be a quarrel among schools of philosophy. What Dougherty seems bent on reviving is not so much philosophy as "integralism" in Catholic theology. For "selective Catholicism" cannot be repressed, and doctrinal orthodoxy enforced, apart from thorough indoctrination in the categories of scholastic philosophy.

The liberals featured in *America*'s symposium for the most part share the same list of issues with their neoconservative colleagues in *Catholicism in Crisis*, but they disagree significantly in their assessment of them. Far from calling for a reassertion of *Humanae vitae*, Sidney Callahan and Charles E. Curran see a thorough revision of the church's teachings on birth control in particular and sexual ethics in general as the key to further progress in renewing the spirit of Vatican II. Virtually all the writers hope that greater scope will be given to freedom of conscience in the church, not less. George G. Higgins is particularly eloquent in recognizing the limits of the "'grand opera' of ecclesiastical life." In words reminiscent of Hecker, he insists that "spiritual renewal lies beyond the scope of administrative acts." On the question of seminary education, Brian O. McDermott, while discussing the same documents as Jude Dougherty, defends the American "Program of Priestly Formation" as a step in the right direction. Apparently unconcerned by Scholastic philosophy's loss of privileged status in the curriculum, McDermott hopes that the Synod will "acknowledge the existence of several models of the church, of the priest and of the seminary." In its explicit departures from the religious praxis of the pre-Conciliar church, the liberal version of "selective Catholicism" thus seems to be deliberate and systematic.

What, then, of collegiality? Do the liberals and neoconservatives differ from each other on this central question as much as they do on the others? Since the neoconservatives regard themselves as defending "the true Vatican II" from the falsehoods perpetrated by the rest of us, they are not about to deny the Council's explicit teaching. Instead, they content themselves with undercutting the American church's ability to institutionalize collegiality in new forms of Catholic religious praxis. Consistent with the overall editorial policy of *Catholicism in Crisis*, Phyllis Zagano, for example, tries to discredit the N.C.C.B. and the U.S.C.C., alleging that the former, characterized as the "left wing of the Democratic party at prayer," is "enslaved in the rhetoric of [the latter's] lay staffers." But the key challenge to the expanding praxis of collegiality is raised, inevitably, by Michael Novak. Among the factors he sees contributing to the post-Conciliar crisis in Catholicism is the very existence of national episcopal conferences:

> Since Vatican II, a new institution has begun to function among the world's bishops: national (or regional) conferences of bishops functioning according to majority votes, in consideration of documents necessarily prepared by administrative staffs. The problems here are twofold: first, increasing nationalism and regionalism, apart from the deep Catholic sense of universality; second, a breakdown in the Catholic system of checks and balances. Theologically, authority on faith and morals is vested in each single bishop, not in a majority vote of conferences of bishops. Once presented with a document in their conferences, it is very hard for individual bishops publicly to dissent. Minority voices are likely to be lost.[19]

The authors of the *America* symposium, one imagines, would find Novak's remark about a "breakdown in the Catholic system of checks and balances" truly astonishing. As they testify with virtual unanimity, the bishops' conferences are but a very modest beginning in creating effective structures of collegiality. Before Vatican II there was no system, Catholic or otherwise, of checks and balances within the church. Instead of curtailing this experiment, the liberals, led by Bishop James Malone, the N.C.C.B.'s current president, are prepared not only to defend the bishops' conferences in general but also to commend "to the church universally . . . the positive experience of our own National Conference of Catholic Bishops . . . ."[20] Rather than wishing to restrict the development of these conferences, the liberals are one in seeking a theology to guide their further expansion in deliberative and consultative processes open to the whole People of God, such as the recent pastoral letter process. This is the context in which to understand their repeated calls for understanding the church's own governance in terms of the principle of "subsidiarity," an idea whose implications we shall explore in chapters five and six. Without actually recognizing it as such, the liberals thus seem already prepared to press on with the church's "New Experiment in Democracy."

In order to understand how both perspectives, liberal and neoconservative, may contribute to the formation of the Americanist agenda, one must be clear about the necessarily selective character of each. For if the one party tends to be openly revisionist while the other claims for itself the mantle of orthodoxy, the polarization between the two is likely to continue, much to the detriment of American Catholicism. Thus it is necessary to take a closer look at the neoconservative view in order to dispel its mistaken claim to orthodoxy, its nostalgia for the lingering illusion of "integralism." For the issue is not a choice, as some neoconservatives would have us believe, between heresy and orthodoxy, but a comparative understanding of a range of "selective Catholicisms," all of which must be challenged in order to stimulate the emergence of an authentically American Catholicism.

Viewed from this angle, the most illuminating neoconservative statement is Michael Novak's *Confession of a Catholic*.[21] For in it Novak reveals the pathos of neoconservatism, its emotional ambivalence over the death of the immigrant church. As the author of a popular tract cheering on the reformers at Vatican II, *The Open Church*,[22] Novak now sees himself recanting his youthful enthusiasm and rallying the church against the excesses of the "radical Catholicism" that he once, apparently, espoused. In deliberate contrast to his earlier critique of conservative bishops at Vatican II as partisans of a "nonhistorical orthodoxy," he now denounces the radicals' heresy of "nonhistorical neodoxy," that is, their eagerness to "update" the church without any appreciation for its unique traditions.[23] The rage, confusion, and guilt of those who feel somehow betrayed by Vatican II seems painfully evident in Novak's heresy-hunting. For in expounding on the Nicene Creed as the litmus test of Catholic orthodoxy, he usually emphasizes his grievances against the majority of American Catholics who seem comfortable in their "selective Catholicism."

The church went wrong after Vatican II, in Novak's current view, when certain popular theologians, including himself, allowed the ancient Trinitarian heresies, now all lumped together as "gnosticism," once more to stifle the church's authentic ethos of incarnationalism. Since virtually everything in the church that he finds ugly and unacceptable derives from this new gnosticism, he is not very tight in defining it. Two issues in particular are evidence of its renewed presence: the prophetic demand for justice toward women in the church raised by Catholic feminists, and the massive repudiation of ecclesiastical authority to bind Catholic consciences in matters of faith and morals. Both of these problems challenge the church's incarnational self-understanding, the latter by denying that, for a Catholic, even spiritual authority must be concretely embodied; the former, by denying the relevance of the divinely mandated differences between the sexes in organizing human society. In addition, gnosticism manifests itself politically in the intellectual vogue that Marxism currently enjoys as the preferred form of "social analysis" among radical Catholic activists. All of these tendencies are gnostic insofar as they appeal to a special "gnosis" or knowledge higher and more authoritative than that codified in the Creed of the church.

In reacting against the feminist form of gnosticism, Novak refuses to de-emphasize the sexual element in the symbolism of the Trinity. The maleness of God the Father and God the Son is not to be clothed in some inoffensively generic identity, for, given Novak's incarnational logic, believers are not to second-guess God's decision to reveal himself in a father's love for his son, but to seek in God's revealed nature the clue to the mysteries of human sexuality. Though Novak begs off discussing the problems of sexism in the church's traditional religious praxis, his defense of the Trinitarian symbolism clearly is meant to put Catholic feminists on the defensive. By associating their aspirations for justice with the ancient church's struggle with gnosticism, in effect Novak is suggesting that everyone sympathetic to the concrete objectives of Catholic feminists, namely, increased opportunity for women to participate in the governance of the church, including the ordained ministry, inevitably must wind up with Mary Daly in denouncing the very idea of the Holy Trinity as sexist.[24]

So far, then, Novak's attack upon gnosticism seems straightforwardly "integralist": he simply refuses to modify the traditional symbols of the Creed in order to accommodate the religious and moral experience of many American Catholics. Ferreting out the gnosticism involved in questioning ecclesiastical authority, however, requires some degree of subtlety. For while Novak may have joined the integralists in repudiating Catholic feminism, he is not yet ready to go along with their defense of *Humanae vitae*. Like the "radicals" whom he opposes, he rejects the substance of Papal teaching on birth control; but he also labors hard to convince his readers that, unlike the radicals', his dissent is loyal to the teaching authority of the church.[25] Having previously unmasked the seductive strategies of the theologians at Vatican II, Novak continues to rely on these very same strategies to legitimate his own dissent. For the arguments that he offers, pointing out both the "inevitably historical" character of the papal teaching and the "tentative, exploratory" nature of his "open" questioning, differ not at all from those produced by

Charles E. Curran and other liberals who have led the way in resisting *Humanae vitae*.[26] At least in this one instance, it is unclear how his attitude of loyal "dialogue" is any different from that of the "selective Catholicism" that he repudiates. The "smoke of Satan" that he claims to see through here is very murky indeed.

Novak's critique of Marxism as the political recrudescence of "gnosticism" is more straightforward. Having recanted his own brief flirtation with the Catholic Left, *A Theology of Radical Politics*,[27] and now armed with the insights of Eric Voegelin and Karl Loewith into the errors of gnosticism and Marxism respectively, Novak sees nothing but mischief in Dom Helder Camara's suggestion that dialogue with Marxism may in our own time be as fruitful theologically as Aquinas' creative reassessment of Aristotle was in the Middle Ages.[28] Gnosticism is to be seen not only in the way "the new Catholic Left" has been seduced by Marxism's false promise of liberation, but also in the "masochism" with which they embrace its "anti-Americanism." So powerful is the hold of gnosticism among the best Catholic theologians, that Novak must even denounce David Tracy for failing to break through the "defensive and guilt-ridden" conventions of Marxist cultural criticism.[29]

In the context of our attempt to recover the liberating possibilities hidden in the Americanist heresy, Novak's remarks on gnosticism and "anti-Americanism" are particularly irresistible. Apparently, Novak believes that his own form of "selective Catholicism" is the only one that can lay claim to the Americanist tradition. Those liberals on the Left, who once marched alongside him for civil rights and against the war in Vietnam, and who still struggle on for participatory democracy not just in the church but also in society as a whole, in his view somehow have forfeited their own claim to patriotism. Novak's attack upon "anti-Americanism" is to function as a taboo to keep others from thinking out the meaning of patriotism in alternative, but still no less Catholic, terms. He apparently holds that the true Americanist Catholic is, like himself, of two minds about democracy, welcoming it whenever it is consistent with his immediate political purposes, but also rejecting it whenever it surfaces in discussions aimed at reforming either the church or the U.S. economy. But a consistently dangerous memory of Americanism should exhibit no such ambivalence: though it may have taken Catholics over a century to realize it, the principle of "self-governing association" is, as I am arguing, just as applicable to religious praxis as it is to secular politics.

Indeed, Novak's brand of Americanism is almost an inversion of the priorities of the original Americanists. Thus, for example, he finds the Americanist tradition useful for bashing the bishops when their pronouncements are not as unguarded as his own in praise of "democratic capitalism."[30] But he passes over that tradition in silence when judging the attempts of these same bishops to display a genuinely American openness toward experiments with freedom within the church. No one who has grasped the essence of the Americanist tradition, its reverence for that "certain liberty" that should mark the way even Catholics relate to each other in this country, would ever endorse Cardinal Ratzinger's attempt to discredit and foreclose the church's most successful experiment in collegiality so far, the regional and national episcopal conferences. Examined in the light of the Americanist tradition, Novak's current confession of Catholicism is not only selective, it is also seriously flawed in its priorities.

Novak's neoconservative alternative to what he designates as the extremes of traditional and radical Catholicism, not surprisingly, shows signs of our ambiguous bereavement over the death of the immigrant church. He thus entirely overestimates the role that he and other popular theologians played in killing the immigrant church. A new generation of educated and independent laity, increasingly distant from the experience of their immigrant ancestors and successful in achieving a new identity as Americans, were already emancipating themselves, long before Novak accomplished his own liberation in an "open church." Young theologians like himself did not create this new generation but they did become popular precisely because they expressed its religious aspirations. Similarly misplaced is Novak's attack upon the methodology of his theological colleagues: what he once celebrated as a triumphant struggle against "nonhistorical orthodoxy" is now regarded as little more than a tawdry conspiracy to subvert the real meaning of Vatican II. Dissent, in Novak's current view, always has the upper hand because the posture of "dialogue" makes those who would reassert the claims of authority look bad in the media.[31] Novak thus accuses progressive theologians of failing to exercise self-discipline, but all they may really be guilty of is failing to share his recently acquired taste for self-castigation.

The marks of bereavement can also be traced in Novak's failure to retain a healthy sense of proportion. Reading his confession provokes the impression that, in his view, the current debate over the church's "option for the poor" is just as symptomatic of "decadence" as the tackiness of so many suburban parish liturgies. No educated Catholic can refuse to acknowledge Novak's feeling that so much of what passes for liturgical reform is, indeed, "torture to the soul."[32] But has he forgotten that the Catholic incarnational principle is working here as leaven in rather meager dough? The shallowness that Novak berates is also typically American, part of the inevitable price to be paid, as he himself has argued elsewhere, for living in the pluralistic but now thoroughly industrialized culture of "democratic capitalism." Yet it is a serious mistake to transfer the "disgust" triggered by culturally impoverished liturgy to the kind of soul-searching demanded by the church's "option for the poor."[33] Granted, this notion stands in need of careful interpretation; thanks to the pastoral letter process, however, it is slowly being transformed into an evangelical challenge that asks Catholics to honor once more the church's commitment to "Liberty and Justice for All." Here, too, the Catholic incarnational principle is acting as leaven, but in a richer dough that is also authentically American: the holy restlessness of a nation whose history has been forged in the crucible of one moral crusade after another. This restlessness, this passion for liberty and justice, is but the bright side of the tacky shallowness that Novak has emphasized. And, like the shallowness, that restlessness is an inescapable part, if anything is, of the ethos of "democratic capitalism."

Novak's private Thermidor might be dismissed as merely a distraction were it not that his views have had significant impact as the bishops' own pastoral letter process has unfolded. Through the vehicle of *Catholicism and Crisis* and the self-appointed lay commissions on Catholic social teaching closely related to it, Novak has transformed his personal struggle into a vocal and well-organized challenge to the bishops' "New American Experiment in Democracy." The challenge is launched, first of all, on appropriately methodological grounds. Invoking philosopher Jacques Maritain's crucial programmatic analysis of "The Structure of Action,"[34] Novak distinguishes between the "spheres of Gospel teaching in human life" in such a way that the bishops would be prohibited from making specific prudential judgments about questions of public policy in their pastoral letters. Here is where he is most innovative in formulating his own version of "selective Catholicism."

Maritain himself, on the basis of a controversial distinction between the spiritual and the temporal "planes" of historical existence, wanted to restrict official church involvement in the ideological struggles tearing Catholic Europe apart during the mid-1930s. He hoped to save the church's worldly mission from the rabid anticlericalism common on all sides of the struggle over communism and fascism. Amidst a controversy among French Catholics specifically addressing the appropriate scope of the Catholic press, he thus proposed a division of labor in Catholic social action that would simultaneously increase the responsible participation of the laity in public affairs while also reducing the church's vulnerability to anticlerical persecution. The two "planes," in Maritain's view, required three distinct strategies of social action: (1) activity on the "spiritual" plane that engages the person "as a Christian as such"; (2) activity on the "temporal" plane in which the person acts merely "as Christian engaging only myself, not the Church"; and (3) an intermediary "zone of truths" where social action involves "the plane of the spiritual considered in its connection with the temporal."[35]

Given these three strategies, the clergy were to restrict their activity to the first and third areas, and leave the second to the laity. Concretely, this meant that on the first level the clergy were to carry out their vocation as teachers and spiritual directors "preparing laymen to act as Christians." But they were also to be active on the third level, especially in situations where together with the laity they had to organize themselves to defend the church's institutional presence in society. Maritain here is actually defending the clergy's role in resisting the encroachments of fascist and other aggressively secular governments seeking to destroy the church's freedom to organize, for example, private Catholic schools and youth organizations. Beyond this crucial area of collaborative political intervention, however, the clergy were not to act and the laity were to act "as Christians" without committing the resources of the institutional church one way or another.

Whatever the wisdom of Maritain's proposal in the politically turbulent 1930s, unlike many other aspects of his work it has not well withstood the test of time. Let me try to point out its theoretical and practical difficulties in an American context.[36] Besides the usual drawbacks involved in making too precise a distinction between the natural and the supernatural dimensions of human existence,[37] Maritain's proposal would have made it impossible for Catholic clergy to march at Selma with their Protestant colleague, Dr. Martin Luther King, impossible for them to involve themselves in various forms of grassroots political organizing, ranging from the Nuclear Freeze referendums to the Right to Life movement. They would, in short, not be able to participate in any direct action giving public witness to their interpretations of Catholic social teaching. This outcome strikes me as self-defeating, for it would sustain and promote a Catholic religious praxis that tends to be artificial in its divisions, and ultimately superstitious in its view of the clergy. Such a distinction, obviously, is completely foreign to the unabashed activism of both clergy and laity in the Americanist tradition.

In Novak's hands, however, Maritain's proposal is pushed even further: the division of labor he has in mind would restrict the clergy's ministry within the church while leaving the laity to minister to the world. Furthermore, this division would be extended beyond the question of social action to the very exercise of teaching authority within the church. The clergy, especially the bishops organized in national episcopal conferences, in his view, are to confine themselves to articulating the principles of Catholic social teaching, and to leave to the laity alone the task of drawing prudential judgments about their implementation. For, according to Novak, Maritain's distinction of "planes" entails a "differentiation of functions and authority" that confines the clergy to teaching only on the first and second levels:

> In the third, the focus of Catholic teaching normally passes from the hands of the bishops and popes to the concrete moral reasoning of individual Catholics responsible for fulfilling their vocations in the world. This is because in the world of contingency and action, church leaders cannot summarize all concrete possibilities, but must enunciate religious ideals and moral principles and demand that lay persons apply them to concrete situations prudently and prayerfully.[38]

A careful reading of Maritain hardly warrants this strange innovation. For Maritain was concerned with "the structure of social action," while Novak is revising the very structure of authority in Catholic social teaching. Examined just on its own merits, however, much of what Novak says in defense of his innovative proposal is true, but beside the point. Of course, church

leaders cannot summarize all concrete possibilities; but that
has hardly made any of them shy in pointing out, to the best of
their abilities, the practical consequences of the principles they
are teaching. Nor should it. The pronouncements of Pope John
Paul II certainly have accepted the risk of moral concreteness,
as has the entire tradition of papal social encyclicals, not to mention the pastoral letters of the American heirarchy, both before
and after the N.C.C.B.'s initiation of open consultation processes. Novak's proposal does not stand or fall on the question of
whether it is appropriate for the clergy to hold political office.
Arguably, he may have good reasons for siding with the current
pope against the Nicaraguan priests active in the Sandinista
government. What is at stake here, however, is not the role conflict possibly involved in trying simultaneously to be a Catholic
priest and a professional politician, but whether the clergy,
especially the bishops, enjoy the discretion necessary to work
their share of the church's teaching ministry effectively.
Novak's proposal, if acted upon consistently, would be more radical than anything ever dreamed up by the partisans of "Call to
Action"; for it would leave the laity without concrete guidance
from their religious leaders as to what the principles of Catholic
social teaching actually entail. It is ironic that Novak, after having chastised others for extremism in the defense of liberty of
conscience, should assert a truly pernicious extremism of his
own. But such is the divided mind of this neoconservative form
of "selective Catholicism."

There is an alternative to both the political activism of the
Sandinista clergy and the ban on practical counsel that Novak
would impose upon the bishops. It is implicit in the Americanist
tradition, and explicit in the remarks of Archbishop Rembert
Weakland which stand at the head of this chapter. At the heart
of this alternative is a commitment to pluralism, not only in society at large but also within the church. Like Novak's proposal, it
intends to respect the variety of gifts bestowed by the Holy
Spirit within the Christian community. But unlike Novak's, it
would not restrict any of the participants in the exercise of these

gifts. As Weakland put it, the bishops must "reflect . . . on the whole — not just the part." They must show the laity what they think their principles mean, not just theoretically but also empirically. They may be wrong in their sense of how the principles apply concretely to complex policy issues; but they must risk formulating these applications, lest the principles, by remaining theoretical, be regarded as inconsequential and ultimately meaningless.

When bishops and clergy are wrong about the empirical dimensions — or, for that matter, about the religious and moral dimensions — of public policy questions, it is the responsibility of laypersons to challenge them in open dialogue. The church is less likely to be harmed by the occasional confusion that public consultation processes might generate, than it is by enforcing episcopal silence "in the world of contingency and action." If this suggestion remains unconvincing, then consider the practices of the Americanist bishops whom Novak is fond of quoting. As the lay commission's letter, "Toward the Future," rightly recalls, John Ireland and his pioneering colleagues were eloquent in their praise of this nation and its institutions.[39] They often went beyond the principles of Catholic social teaching, and boldly proclaimed, in Ireland's words, that God had "assigned to America . . . a singular mission . . . , the mission of bringing about a new social and political order, based more than any other upon the common brotherhood of man, and more than any other securing to the multitude of the people social happiness and equality of rights."[40]

Whether Ireland's insight into the promise of American institutions is valid or not, I must insist that every such declaration, not to mention his partisan intervention in the politics surrounding U.S. participation in the Spanish-American War of 1898,[41] involves a host of debatable prudential judgments "in the world of contingency and action." If Novak is serious in making such judgments the exclusive responsibility of the Catholic laity, then consistency would seem to require him to stop trying to influence the laity by quoting selectively from the prudential judgments of the Americanist bishops. Alternatively, he might abandon his misguided proposal, and encourage the whole church, including the N.C.C.B., to be as generous and boldly visionary in their prudential judgments today as the Americanist bishops were a century ago.

The polarization between liberal and neoconservative versions of "selective Catholicism" might fruitfully be resolved, were the bishops to seize the initiative and renew the church's identification with its own authentically Americanist tradition. Within the tradition of Hecker and Murray, and of Ireland and Gibbons, there is ample room to affirm the partial insights of both groups. Fortified by the Americanist legacy, Catholic liberals might discover that they need not uncritically accept every anti-American sentiment emanating from the Third World in giving voice to their authentically prophetic impulse for justice in the church and society. Fortified by this same legacy, neoconservatives might discover that American pluralism is a reality that cannot be kept out of the church, and that an adult moral dialogue, in which everyone admits that no one is in a position to call for a pre-emptive strike from Rome, is the only way that such pluralism can be kept from degenerating into chaos. In short, what all of us might discover in the Americanist tradition is a reawakened sense of participation in our common struggle to renew the church after Vatican II.

So far, then, I've been preparing you to accept my interpretation of the church's "New American Experiment in Democracy" by taking you on a tour of American Catholicism's remote and recent history. Out of the papal condemnation of the Americanist heresy I've tried to create a dangerous memory, in order that the hopes and fears awakened by the pastoral letter process can be fully understood. I've tried to provoke fresh thinking on the meaning of Vatican II by suggesting that our current hopes of exercising a "certain liberty" in the church are a result of tasting forbidden fruit: we have already gone a long way in extending the practice of collegiality beyond the college of bishops — so why not, as "Call to Action" recommended, proceed to a full-blown experiment in democracy within the church? In this chapter, I have analyzed the contemporary phenomenon of "selective Catholicism," the ambiguous reality of which may be compared to the symptoms that often accompany our adventures with other kinds of forbidden fruit. I have emphasized its pervasiveness, not only among liberals who are unashamed of it, but also among neoconservatives who apparently are aware of everyone's complicity in "selective Catholicism" except their own. This point must be made, if we are to redeem the "New Experiment in Democracy's" promise for overcoming the polarization and fragmentation present not only in the Catholic church but also in American society as a whole. Thus taking our bearings from these three points in American Catholic history, we may now be in a position to sketch a practical theology for the church's "New Experiment in Democracy."

Notes

1. Jay Dolan, *The American Catholic Experience: A History from Colonial Times to the Present* (Garden City, New York: Doubleday, 1985), p. 192.

2. Eugene Kennedy, *The Now and Future Church: The Psychology of Being an American Catholic* (Garden City, New York: Doubleday, 1984), p. 4.

3. Andrew Greeley, *American Catholics: A Social Portrait* (New York: Basic Books, 1977), p. 50-68.

4. Cf. Kennedy, *op. cit.*; cf. Michael Harrington, *The Politics at God's Funeral: The Spiritual Crisis of Western Civilization* (New York: Viking Penguin Books, 1985).

5. Greeley, *op. cit.*, p. 71.

6. Cf. Andrew Greeley, *American Catholics since the Council: An Unauthorized Report* (Chicago: Thomas More Press, 1985). While Greeley's data does not include specific representation of trends within the Hispanic Catholic communities in this country, this problem clearly does not invalidate what he has to say about the rest of us.

7. *Ibid.*, p. 71.

8. Cf. Robert Blair Kaiser, *The Politics of Sex and Religion* (Kansas City, Missouri: Leaven Press, 1985).

9. Greeley, *American Catholics since the Council*, p. 58-69.

10. *Ibid.*, p. 94.

11. *Ibid.*, p. 95.

12. *Ibid.*, p. 96-7.

13. *Ibid.*, p. 96.

14. *Ibid.*, p. 69; cf. Kaiser, *op. cit.*

15. Cf. The discussions of "The Extraordinary Synod" by James Malone, George G. Higgins, Ladislas Orsy, Avery Dulles, Sidney Callahan, Joan D. Chittister, Charles E. Curran, Monika K. Hellwig, Brian O. McDermott, and Michael J. Buckley in *America* (September 28, 1985), pp. 148-74.

16. Cf. "The Coming Extraordinary Synod: A Symposium," with essays by Robert Royal, Michael Novak, Christopher Wolfe, George A. Kelly, Phyllis Zagano, Benedict M. Ashley, Jude P. Dougherty, Richard R. Roach, James T. O'Connor, and Ronald Lawler in *Catholicism in Crisis*, Vol. 3, No. 7 (May 1985), pp. 10-19.

17. Joseph Cardinal Ratzinger with Vittorio Messori, *The Ratzinger Report: An Exclusive Interview on the State of the Church* (San Francisco: Ignatius Press, 1985). Cardinal Ratzinger is the Prefect of the Vatican's "Sacred Congregation for the Doctrine of the Faith," formerly known as the Holy Office or the Inquisition.

18. Jude P. Dougherty, *art. cit.*, in *Catholicism in Crisis*, p. 16.

19. Michael Novak, *art. cit.*, in *Catholicism in Crisis*, p.11.

20. James Malone, *art. cit.*, in *America*, p. 150.

21. Michael Novak, *Confession of a Catholic* (San Francisco: Harper and Row, 1983).

22. Michael Novak, *The Open Church, Vatican II, Act II* (New York: Macmillan, 1964).

23. Novak, *Confession of a Catholic*, p. 46.

24. Cf. Mary Daly, *Beyond God the Father: Toward a Philosophy of Women's Liberation* (Boston: Beacon Press, 1973).

25. Novak, *Confession of a Catholic*, p. 125.

26. *Ibid.*, p. 112.

27. Michael Novak, *A Theology for Radical Politics* (New York: Herder and Herder, 1969).

28. Novak, *Confession of a Catholic*, p. 174; cf. Helder Camara, "What Would St. Thomas Aquinas, the Aristotle Commentator, Do If Faced with Karl Marx?" in David Tracy, ed., *Celebrating the Medieval Heritage: A Colloquy on the Thought of Aquinas and Bonaventure*, in *The Journal of Religion*, Vol. 78 (Chicago: University of Chicago Press, 1978), pp. S174-82.

29. Novak, *Confession of a Catholic*, p. 180-1.

30. Michael Novak, "Blaming America: A Comment on Paragraphs 202-204 of the First Draft," in *Catholicism in Crisis*, Vol. 3, No. 8 (July, 1985), pp. 12-6.

31. Novak, *Confession of a Catholic*, p. 113.

32. *Ibid.*, p. 87.

33. Cf. *Ibid.*, pp. 164-9; cf. Michael Novak's *Freedom with Justice: Catholic Social Thought and Liberal Institutions* (San Francisco: Harper and Row, 1984), which presents a more measured interpretation of the "option for the poor," p. 192.

34. Jacques Maritain, "The Structure of Action," pp. 291-308, in *Integral Humanism: Temporal and Spiritual Problems of a New Christendom* (Notre Dame: University of Notre Dame Press, 1973); cf. Michael Novak, *Moral Clarity in the Nuclear Age* (Nashville, Tennessee: Thomas Nelson Publishers, 1983), p. 27-28.

35. Cf. Maritain, *op. cit.*, pp. 294, 296.

36. For an analysis of Maritain's proposal parallel to my own, cf. Gustavo Gutierrez, *A Theology of Liberation* (Maryknoll, New York: Orbis Books, 1973), pp. 53-77.

37. Cf. Henri de Lubac, *The Mystery of the Supernatural* (New York: Herder and Herder, 1967).

38. Novak, *Moral Clarity in the Nuclear Age*, p. 28.

39. Lay Commission on Catholic Social Teaching and the U.S. Economy, *Toward the Future: A Lay Letter* (New York: American Catholic Committee, 1984), pp. 7-17.

40. *Ibid.*, p. 14.

41. Cf. James Hennesey, S. J., *American Catholics: A History of the Roman Catholic Community in the United States* (New York: Oxford University Press, 1981), p. 202.

4

PUBLIC DIALOGUE: THE GROUND RULES FOR A COMMUNITY OF MORAL DISCOURSE

Even within the limits of legitimate pluralism there are important truth claims involved in the positions taken. One should strive to convince others of the truth of one's own position, but one cannot claim than an opposing position places one outside the church. Since there are a number of legitimate positions within the church, the church itself must often be seen as a community of moral discourse, rather than as a provider of answers for its members in all such cases.

— Charles E. Curran, "Catholic Teaching on Peace and War," in *Directions in Catholic Social Ethics*.

A theology for a "New American Experiment in Democracy" cannot be built simply on the dangerous memories of Catholics still struggling with the death of the immigrant church. It must also be anchored in the mainstream of American Christianity as a whole. Defining the historic essence of Christianity in America is an almost impossible task; but no effort to do so has yet surpassed H. Richard Niebuhr's essay, *The Kingdom of God in America*.[1] Like Catholics seeking to identify with the Americanist tradition, Niebuhr was impressed, even bewildered, by the pluralism of religious praxis in this country. Just as ardently as any neoconservative Catholic, he feared the fragmentation and hence the trivialization of Christianity, not just for the sake of the church but also because of its destructive consequences for American society as a whole. But unlike the neoconservatives, he did not look for a papal intervention to resolve our indigenous problems with pluralism, but tried to discern historically the underlying pattern of American Christian experience. He hoped that an appreciation of this pattern might help Christians — Catholics as well as Protestants — give public witness more effectively to their common faith. His goal and method, obviously, are similar to those animating this book.

In Niebuhr's view, American Christianity is best understood as "a movement which finds its center in the faith in the kingdom of God."[2] Many theologians, especially in the Protestant social gospel tradition, had defined a similar starting point before; but Niebuhr's view was distinctive for its awareness of the changing character of this faith, both from one historical period to another and from one religious community to another. Out of this diversity he generalized three basic perspectives responding to the movement of Christianity in this country:

> In the early period of American life, when foundations were laid upon which we have all had to build, "kingdom of God" meant "sovereignty of God": in the creative period of awakening and revival it meant "reign of Christ"; and only in the most recent period had it come to mean "kingdom on earth."[3]

The interaction betwen these three meanings, then, accounts for the dynamism of American Christianity. In the current phase of its movement, the church is still wrestling with the legacy of the social gospel: it is still seeking to understand what it means to establish the "kingdom on earth" without institutionalizing idolatries that would, in effect, deny either the "sovereignty of God" or the "reign of Christ." A half century after Niebuhr offered this analysis, there's no reason to suppose that American Christianity has resolved the problem posed by seeking the "kingdom on earth."

American Catholicism's "New Experiment in Democracy," I submit, is best understood as part of this larger movement toward realizing the "kingdom on earth." In the past fifty years since Niebuhr wrote, or to be more precise, in the past twenty years, the Catholic movement in this country, for better or for worse, has converged toward the Protestant mainstream. Catholic religious praxis, like Protestant, now requires a theology of the Kingdom of God in America. But unlike Niebuhr's, inevitably it will remain distinctively Catholic. Ironically, Niebuhr himself provides the best clue as to how it will do so. In light of his own contrast between the essence of American Christianity, epitomized as the quest for the "Kingdom of God," and Catholicism's perennial focus on the "vision of God,"[4] it becomes apparent that what American Catholicism might contribute to the theology of the Kingdom is more penetrating insight into the reality of God, or, if you will, a theology of the Divine Life animating the movement of Christianity in America.

When Niebuhr's triad of interrelated meanings for the "Kingdom of God" is examined in light of Isaac Hecker's vision of God, its unmistakably Trinitarian significance virtually leaps from the pages. The "sovereignty of God," of course, refers to the universal sustaining activity of the One whom Jesus called Father; and the "reign of Christ" emphasizes the embodiment of the Son in structures of redemption, beginning with the church. But in the work of building the "kingdom on earth," Hecker and the Americanists would have recognized the continuing activity of the Holy Spirit, not just in the structures of the church but in individual believers, in their fellow citizens, and in the unfolding of their common destiny as a nation. Identifying with the Americanist tradition, then, requires the development of a theological perspective that will sharpen the capacities of Catholics for discerning the presence of the Holy Spirit in the "kingdom on earth."

In the chapters that follow, I hope to propose such a perspective: first, by describing how it is that the church is preparing itself to participate in this work by becoming a "community of moral discourse"; second, by showing how the Trinitarian vision of God suggests the proper manner of building the "kingdom on earth," under the rubric of "justice as participation"; and finally, by reading "the signs of the times" as they illuminate what this vision of God and human community may mean for American society today. All three of these elements, I contend, are present in the church's "New Experiment in Democracy." All three have surfaced in the Catholic bishops' pastoral letter process; here I am merely trying to identify them and give them a coherent theological focus.

Let us begin by examining the church's resources for becoming a community of moral discourse. James M. Gustafson, the Protestant mentor of so many of today's American Catholic ethicists, formulated this notion in order to stress the church's "lay and voluntary character."[5] Gustafson, of course, was focusing on the way in which the principle of "self-governing association" has continually influenced the religious praxis of all the Christian denominations in this country, including Catholicism. Under the religious inspiration of the left wing of the Reformation, the American experiment with separation of church and state has changed inherited structures of religious community, especially the way the *sensus fidelium* freely forming the community is sustained as a moral consensus. As we have seen, the genius of the Americanist tradition consists in its openness to the religious implications of this experiment, not just as a matter of expediency but as testimony to the transforming presence of the Holy Spirit in the Catholic church.

In pluralistic America, even the Catholic church, if it is to survive the passing of the immigrant generations, cannot help but become a community of moral discourse. For such a community, in Gustafson's words, becomes "a gathering of people with the explicit intention to survey and critically discuss their personal and social responsibilities in the light of moral convictions about which there is some consensus and to which there is some loyalty."[6] Gustafson is not saying that such discussion is the only function of the church; he is saying that in a pluralistic society, which by definition shares no deep consensus about either moral convictions or social responsibilities, the churches must clear the space in which those gathered together can come to know their own minds and govern themselves accordingly. By calling the church "a community of moral discourse," he is suggesting not just a range of topics for discussion, but the nature of the process by which consensus about them may be reached.

Given our interest in identifying this process in its distinctively American Catholic form, three points made by Gustafson will be crucial for our own reflections. First, the discourse by definition must be moral, as opposed to "therapeutic."[7] Though the contrast between the two can be overstated, Gustafson here is warning the church that, even in a pluralistic society — rather, especially in a pluralistic society — it must not acquiesce in the "privatization" of its worldly mission. Moral discourse in the church, at least, is not focused primarily on private questions of "self-fulfillment," but on the public "direction of human activity, in light of an understanding of what is right and wrong, what is better and worse."[8] Churches characteristically achieve this public focus and continually resist privatization by re-examining the validity of their distinctive traditions of moral wisdom, founded upon, but not exclusively rooted in, the Bible.

Gustafson's second point is that to be a community of moral discourse the church must institutionalize disciplined "ethical reflection" upon its traditions. Ethical reflection means simply the kind of careful attention to the logic of moral argument that usually results from serious study of "the questions . . . [discussed] in the history of Western ethical thought." Granted its public focus, if the churches' moral discourse is not to degenerate into ideological warfare, then intellectuals loyal to each religious community must lead the way in helping other participants to clarify its "fundamental principles and convictions," to criticize the truth claims supporting the "moral authority of . . . [this particular] body of doctrine," and in applying these principles to determine "why one course of action is better than another, one judgment better than another."[9] The danger of ideological fragmentation can be minimized, in other words, if religious intellectuals act as facilitators who teach the rest of us the basic skills necessary for the intelligent use of the community's "moral language."

Gustafson's third point is implicit in the other two, namely, that the entire community must participate in the process of consensus formation, or else there will be no true consensus. The church must become a true "congregation," that is, "a place of speaking and hearing" in which all participants share in discerning "God's will . . . for this gathering of his people."[10] While Gustafson recognizes the indispensable role of expertise in such a process, he also insists that consensus "is shortcut by virtue of the absence of persons who must bear the consequences of action." The role of the minister in sustaining a community of moral discourse thus is analogous to that of the political leader in a participatory democracy. He or she is "responsive to the consensus that exists . . . , but . . . is also the shaper of the consensus." The minister's moral authority, of course, depends upon the quality of his or her response to the community's emerging moral consensus: "He may not know all the data that a politician knows, but he may be able to reshape the questions which bring technical data into social policy and moral action by his own moral sensibility and his practiced moral deliberations."[11]

In defending his notion of the church as a community of moral discourse, Gustafson notes its obvious precedents in the Protestant religious praxis of colonial New England. Nevertheless, his proposal is clearly and emphatically open to development by the Catholic community in pluralistic America. Indeed, while the American Catholic church heretofore may have been deficient in the degree of participation involved in its processes of consensus formation, Gustafson praises it for its rich tradition of moral discourse and its usually careful attention to the rigors of ethical reflection.[12] While Gustafson commends these Catholic strengths to American Protestants, here I must reciprocate by pointing out how Protestantism's participatory style may hold the key to Catholicism's future development as a community of moral discourse. Seen in this context, the Catholic bishops' pastoral letter process, indeed, is very promising.

Were the elements identified by Gustafson in his model of the church merely the artifacts of American Protestant tradition, their appearance within the pastoral letter process could be construed as one more Catholic capitulation to "indifferentism." But, as John Courtney Murray already seems to have grasped in the discussion of "civility" that we reviewed in chapter two, what is at stake in the notion of a community of moral discourse is a normative view of human association in general. The Swiss Catholic theologian, Hans Küng, in his own way, recognized the ecclesial significance of this norm in his neglected book, *Truthfulness: the Future of the Church*. Responding to the distress caused by the publication of *Humanae vitae*, Küng identified "truthfulness" with the Biblical virtue of *parrhesia*, or the "candour before God and man," that makes each individual believer "unembarrassedly frank, utterly fearless" in his or her pursuit of the truth.[13] More sharply provocative than Murray's "civility," Küng's "truthfulness" lends a note of urgency to this normative view of human association: making it the cornerstone of Catholic religious praxis will inevitably create conditions that lead either to chaos or to the formation of a community of moral discourse. In order to clarify the normative view of human association implicit in the exhortations of both Murray and Küng, we need to consider briefly the ideal of a rational society proposed by the German social theorist, Jürgen Habermas.

At the core of Habermas' theory is the notion that human community ought to be, as it essentially is, "a truth-dependent mode of socialization."[14] For unless the basic institutional routines which shape our lives — in other words, the "socialization" processes — are truth-dependent, there's no point in trying to determine the moral consensus that underlies them. To be "truth-dependent," however, is to rest upon truth: institutional routines, according to Habermas, cannot logically justify themselves. Since they are inevitably susceptible to corruption, they offer no intrinsic guarantee of their own relationship to the truth. There must be something in the nature of human association that makes "civility" and "truthfulness" not only desirable but possible, something in the deep structure of human communication in general that requires communities of moral discourse to be genuinely truth-dependent. In Habermas' terms, there must be a pattern of "communicative competence" operative in any form of human association as such.

Habermas argues in favor of this presupposition on the basis of what he takes to be the nature of normal human interaction and the truth-claims implicit in it. The crucial question is how do people successfully communicate, let alone achieve consensus, about anything? The Anglo-American philosophers, J. L. Austin and John Searle, gave Habermas the necessary clue in their theory of "speech acts," that is, in their recognition that any successful human utterance contains a certain "illocutionary force," which, according to Habermas, establishes the ground rules by which speakers and their hearers can test their respective truth-claims.[15] In general such truth-claims fall into certain logical patterns which Strain and I in *Polity and Praxis* — following Habermas — typify as "adequacy," "appropriateness," and "authenticity."[16] The details of the theory need not concern us here.[17] Our focus is limited to Habermas' contention that the speech acts generating these claims presuppose "an ideal speech situation," which, though it is never fully realized in the institutional routines of particular forms of human association, does provide the norms for any "truth-dependent mode of socialization" whatsoever. If it can be validated, Habermas's theory of "communicative competence" thus specifies the formal and universal conditions necessary for any group to act as a community of moral discourse.

For the ideal speech situation implicit in the successful performance of ordinary "speech acts" provides the space in which disagreements generated in the course of human interaction may give rise to public dialogue as a process of consensus formation. Formally considered, public dialogue occurs when discussion among people representing a diversity of perspectives — even conflicting perspectives — is structured so that only "the peculiarly forceless force of better arguments" can determine its outcome.[18] Public dialogue thus occurs in a context of generalized "communicative competence": having mastered the force of their own speech acts, all the participants have an equal chance to influence the outcome of the discussion through criticism of each other's truth-claims, specifically, the adequacy of each other's factual assertions, the appropriateness of each other's recommendations for action, and the authenticity of each other's intentions. Consensus in public dialogue is reached when all participants can agree that any relevant questions regarding these truth-claims have found acceptable answers.

Habermas's ideal description of "truth-dependent mode[s] of socialization" helps clarify each of the three characteristics of a community of moral discourse identified by Gustafson. First, regarding the contrast between "moral" and "therapeutic" discourse, Habermas affirms the distinction but does not rule out important relationships between the two. In particular, by contrasting the possibility of "systematically distorted communication" with the operations of normal human interaction, Habermas establishes an indispensable but preliminary role for "therapeutic" discourse in the formation of a true consensus. In order to form a community of moral discourse, participants must always be ready to cross-examine the various ideologies distorting their capacities to enter into public dialogue,[19] a task which Habermas, following the Frankfurt School of critical social theory, sees as essentially therapeutic. Approaching the problem of ideological distortion in this way, Habermas thus corrects Gustafson's mistaken assumption that "therapeutic" discourse is limited primarily to personal questions. The churches will better realize their own nature as communities of moral discourse, not by ignoring the therapeutic dimension but by transforming it into a self-imposed penitential discipline, an instrument for minimizing the impact of the ideological biases of all those who would attempt to discern the will of God for the community.

Regarding Gustafson's second point, which asserts the need for disciplined ethical reflection and the role of religious intellectuals in facilitating it, Habermas's theory shows how the move from moral exhortation to ethical reflection is merely one crucial instance of the movement from praxis to theory implicit in the performative logic of all speech acts. In this view, there is nothing particularly Catholic — or Protestant, for that matter — about recourse to disciplined ethical reflection. Such reflection, as we shall see, simply renders the community's particular tradition of moral wisdom accountable to the formal, universal norms implicit in any "truth-dependent mode of socialization." Habermas' formal description of communicative competence in moral discourse, in effect, generates procedures of ethical reflection no different from the "natural law" tradition of religious ethics in mainstream Protestant, as well as Catholic, churches.[20] Moreover, once such procedures are understood as implicit in the notion of communicative competence and therefore available to all participants in public dialogue, religious intellectuals will have no other choice but to act as facilitators in the formation of a community of moral discourse. They can no longer pretend to be its arbiters. For to the extent that it actually is a "truth-dependent mode of socialization," the community will know no *traditio arcana*, no special gnosis unavailable to ordinary participants, and will grant no privilege in moral discourse to any perspective not warranted by "the peculiarly forceless force of better arguments."

Habermas supports Gustafson's third point, which defends the participation of all members of the community in the process of consensus formation, by insisting on the equality of all participants in opportunities to influence the outcome of a public dialogue. Like Gustafson, Habermas recognizes the "counterfactual" nature of this norm, namely, that its implementation must necessarily be limited by certain empirical conditions found in virtually every form of human organization, including "lay and voluntary" associations. I refer to the universal human phenomenon of leadership, and the exercise of authority based on credentials or recognized achievements. As we have seen in the preceding chapters, the churches' public witness requires a skillful blend of professional and religious competence, responsive to the distinctive contours of the community's historic traditions. Habermas' theory, nevertheless, rightly creates a permanent suspicion against any notions of specialized competence, or religious authority and technical expertise, not ultimately grounded in the generalized "communicative competence" possessed in principle by all participants in the community. Consistent with this theory, Gustafson would stimulate the growth of churches as communities of moral discourse by enjoining their ministers to take special care that all relevant perspectives be fairly represented; Habermas would goad us in the same direction more explicitly by rejecting any public consensus not achieved through some form of participatory democracy.

When we turn from these normative considerations to an analysis of the Catholic bishops' pastoral letter process, we see reasons to be cautiously optimistic, not just because of the unprecedented levels of lay participation it has provoked but also because of the way in which the letters' teachings have been structured in order to encourage public dialogue. By contrast, one of the defects of pastoral letters previously issued by the bishops was that ordinary Catholics generally had no sense of identification with them.Typically, they were written by committees made up of staff persons from the U.S.C.C. and then after fairly perfunctory discussion among the bishops, voted on and promulgated in behalf of the N.C.C.B. as a whole. The process, in other words, was not public; and although the content of the letters themselves was often responsive to the shifting mood of public opinion within the church, the laity did not formally participate in the discussion of policies affecting them. As a result, though some activist groups might express dissent, ordinary Catholics usually didn't even bother to protest: once the letters were published, typically they were simply ignored.

The breakthrough, at least partially overcoming this defect, happened almost by accident. While the process of consulting experts in various fields had already been established in preparing the first draft of the pastoral letter, "The Challenge of Peace," public participation began only after the contents of that draft were leaked to the press.[21] For a number of reasons, the N.C.C.B. chose not to turn the leak into a Catholic version of the Daniel Ellsberg case, but published the full text of the draft, thus extending to all who had an interest in it the same invitation for critical response that heretofore they had restricted to the experts. Most likely this decision was not based on considerations of theological principle, but in hindsight it was decisive in opening up the pastoral letter process and making that process itself a model for the church's becoming a community of moral discourse.

After the first draft of "The Challenge of Peace" was leaked, all subsequent drafts of it and the letter on the economy have been submitted routinely to the public for discussion. The coverage given them in the nation's news media, of course, has varied according to the shifting preoccupations of public opinion. While subsequent drafts of "The Challenge of Peace" gained prominent attention as this nation wrestled with the Nuclear Freeze movement and the Euromissile crisis, the diminishing coverage of the second and third drafts of the economic letter apparently has reflected the normal rhythms of U.S. electoral politics. By contrast, its first draft, along with the so-called Lay Commission's letter, "Toward the Future," were newsworthy when they were published in November 1984, because they came as a reprise to the policy debates surrounding the Presidential election. But the second draft, issued in October 1985, and the third, which appeared in June of 1986, lacking direct correlation with the "news" of the day, were given only scant attention. This pattern suggests that, although Andrew Greeley is surely right to emphasize the role of the nation's news media in disseminating the pastoral letters' teachings, the bishops' neoconservative critics are also right to raise questions about what it is actually that the media are disseminating.

As Philip Lawler has pointed out in his summary of the neoconservative complaint against the pastoral letter process, "How Bishops Decide: An American Catholic Case Study," only the final draft of any pastoral letter, the one actually approved by a vote of the N.C.C.B. as a whole, has any religious and moral authority for Catholics.[22] Yet, given the emerging and probably predictable pattern of media coverage, the final draft is least likely to get a detailed examination in the press, whereas the first draft tends to receive the most attention. Whatever the reasons for these media dynamics, they should be a matter of concern — and not just to neoconservatives — because the first draft, with only the initial stages of the consultation behind it, is least likely to reflect the opinions of all participants in the public dialogue. If ordinary Catholics assume that preliminary drafts as reported in the media fully reflect the church's moral consensus, they may be seriously mistaken.

Nevertheless, the answer to neoconservatives like Lawler is not to dismantle the pastoral letter process, but to encourage the church's own agencies to do a better job of presenting the letters, instead of relying on the vagaries of media coverage. The answer, in short, entails greater participation on the part of ordinary Catholics, not less; and as much public dialogue after the letters are approved, as before. However the bishops stumbled into the process, its potential contribution to the quality of the church's moral discourse cannot be underestimated. What with the thousands of pieces of correspondence directed to the drafting committees, the countless assemblies both inside and outside Catholic institutions debating the pastoral letters' merits, and the torrent of literature generated not only in Catholic periodicals, the process itself ought to ensure the widest possible representation of relevant perspectives.

Lawler, however, is not convinced that it does. He regards the pastoral letter process as flawed, not just because of the dynamics of media coverage but because of a certain "ideological predisposition" in the drafting committee itself. The members of the bishops' committee for the letter on the economy were not selected with a view toward representing a range of opinion on specific policy questions. Lacking the diversity of perspectives reflected in the previous committee's work by the presence of both a pacifist, like Bishop Thomas Gumbleton, and a military chaplain, like Cardinal John O'Connor, the bishops working on the economic letter have failed to seek testimony from certain key conservative thinkers, and have ignored the advice given by the few whom they have heard. Lawler insists that these alleged slights are entirely consistent with the overwhelmingly liberal orientation not only of the U.S.C.C. staff and consultants, but also of the bishops serving on the committee. His charges could be set aside as only so much sour grapes, were it not for the warnings given by Gustafson and Habermas that any consensus is only as good as the participation in the process shaping it is inclusive. Who's invited and who's not is just as decisive as the flow of the argument among those that actually get a chance to speak.

Though Gustafson and Habermas probably had in mind the exclusion of the inarticulate poor rather than well-connected neoconservatives, their insistence upon an equality of chances to participate, if it is to be taken seriously, must be applied evenhandedly. Answering Lawler's charges thus requires another look at the appendices to the drafts of the pastoral letter, which list by name not only the consultants and the staff assisting the bishops, but also the dates of the hearings and the names and affiliations of those who appeared before the committee to give testimony. The lists are striking for their inclusiveness, social and occupational, if not ideological: there one finds not just the kinds of credentialed experts, economists, labor leaders, business executives, politicians, theologians and ethicists, whom one would expect to hear from, but also homemakers, grassroots community leaders, budding entrepreneurs, and social visionaries, who are often marginalized for their lack of standing in the country's established elites. It is clear that some of the hearings, especially the one hosted by the Archdiocese of Oakland, California and the University of California at

Berkeley in May 1984, were more successful than others in achieving inclusiveness. But, overall, it cannot be said that any significant social and occupational group was excluded. Nor does the list indicate that the bishops only heard from those who shared their "ideological predisposition." Michael Novak, for example, was their most frequent witness, giving testimony at three different hearings. If Lawler wishes to claim that the bishops are captive to the allegedly unrepresentative opinions of house liberals at the U.S.C.C., he certainly cannot ascribe their waywardness to Novak's lack of opportunities to present opposing views.

Just as important as its promise in securing a breadth of participation, the pastoral letter process is developing a structured format of ethical reflection that allows for both the achievement of consensus on moral principles and the airing of reasonable differences of opinion regarding the interpretation of these principles.[23] At the Notre Dame conference, previously discussed in chapter two, the panel on employment, for example, featured speakers who differed among themselves on the respective roles of business, labor, and government in overcoming unemployment: Joseph A. Pichler, President of Dillon Companies, Rudy Oswald, Director of the AFL-CIO's Department of Economic Research, and former U.S. Secretary of Labor, F. Ray Marshall.[24] David Hollenbach, who later became one of the official consultants to the bishops' committee, gave a paper, "Unemployment and Jobs: A Theological and Ethical Perspective," in which he proposed a framework for thinking about this issue, consistent with the traditions of Catholic social teaching. While Hollenbach's contributions were later to be canonized in the first draft of the pastoral letter, important here is the way in which the panel at which he spoke allowed the bishops'committee not only to get a feel for the complexity of the problems involved in creating and sustaining conditions of full employment, but also to make distinctions between what Catholic social teaching essentially must affirm about human dignity and the diversity of informed conclusions that could reasonably be drawn from it. The structure, in short, allowed for both consensus formation and the recognition of reasonable grounds for competent dissent; and both are indispensable, obviously, if a community of moral discourse is to flourish.

The bishops' decision to prepare the pastoral letters in a process of public dialogue probably would have opened up the possibility for competent dissent in any case. But it was another accident, the unforeseen intervention of the Vatican in the drafting of "The Challenge of Peace," that led to the bishops' structuring their teaching and the pedagogy for it in a way that invites the church to become a community of moral discourse. In January 1983, Archbishop John Roach, at that time the President of the N.C.C.B., and Cardinal-elect Joseph Bernadin, the chairman of the drafting committee for the pastoral letter, along with two key advisers, met with the Prefect of the Vatican's Congregation of the Faith, Cardinal Joseph Ratzinger, the Vatican Secretary of State, Cardinal Agostino Casaroli, and their advisers, as well as representatives of the national episcopal conferences of the nations of western Europe. The meeting was requested by officials at the Vatican after the first and second drafts of the letter had raised various concerns among the western European bishops. Though the meeting was closed to the press, once again a providential leak, this time a memorandum prepared by Jan Schotte, Secretary of the Pontifical Commission on Justice and Peace, summarizing the minutes of the meeting, gives us crucial insight into these concerns and the American bishops' response to them.[25]

The meeting was called because certain bishops in western Europe feared that the American pastoral letter would offer ethical reflection on the morality of nuclear deterrence and the first use of nuclear weapons at odds with their own declarations. Instead of addressing the substance of these important policy issues, the meeting turned on certain procedural questions involved in the religious praxis of American Catholicism, specifically, the American bishops' custom of publishing pastoral letters that did more than restate general principles of Catholic social teaching, and their right (*mandatum docendi*) to issue such letters not as individual bishops, but as a national episcopal conference. In particular, Ratzinger expressed concern that the church's unity of faith might be compromised by the appearance of pluralism in Catholic social teaching.

Ironically, the clarification of the American bishops' teaching authority that Ratzinger accepted may have the effect of stimulating the development of legitimate pluralism within the church. For in view of the traditional Catholic premise that church teaching does bind the consciences of believers, the American bishops were asked to make distinctions among the various levels of episcopal authority standing behind their teachings, and to attach these distinctions quite specifically to the recommendations the pastoral letter offers on policy issues. Since the American bishops were not about to stop issuing pastoral letters, the Vatican sought to impose these distinctions as a way of minimizing the "confusion" that specific policy recommendations might inspire among ordinary Catholics. Whatever Cardinal Ratzinger's intentions, the proposed distinctions could become a magna charta for dissent within the church.

In the final form given them in "The Challenge of Peace," these distinctions make explicit three different levels of authoritative teaching and three corresponding levels of moral obligation. They also imply that moral discourse proceeds with a different focus at each level. The three different levels are described as (1) "universal moral principles," (2) "formal Church teaching," and (3) "prudential judgments." Here is the way the pastoral letter uses these distinctions to establish the ground rules for legitimate dissent:

> We do not intend that our treatment of each of these issues carry the same moral authority as our statement of universal moral principles and formal Church teaching. Indeed we stress here at the beginning that not every statement in this letter has the

same moral authority. At times we reassert universally binding moral principles. At still other times we
reaffirm the statements of recent popes and the
teachings of Vatican II. Again, at other times, we
apply moral principles to specific cases.

When making applications of these principles we
realize — and we wish readers to recognize — that
prudential judgments are involved based on specific
circumstances which can change or which can be interpreted differently by people of good will (e.g., the
treatment of "no first use"). However, the moral judgments that we make in specific cases, while not binding in conscience, are to be given serious attention
and consideration by Catholics as they determine
whether their moral judgments are consistent with
the Gospel.[26]

They reinforce this statement with a promise "to indicate stylis-
tically and substantively, whenever we make such applications," and they invoke Vatican II's Pastoral Constitution,
Gaudium et Spes,[27] as allowing within the church "a certain diversity of views even though all hold the same universal moral
principles." Finally, in order to maintain the unity of faith
within this legitimate pluralism, they stress that "not only conviction and commitment are needed in the Church, but also
civility and charity." In clearing a space for legitimate dissent,
the bishops thus have been led to rediscover the theological insights of both Hecker and Murray.

Each of these three levels requires further explanation if
their role in renewing the American Catholic church as a community of moral discourse is to be fully appreciated. "Universal
moral principles" refers to that body of ethical discernment that
Catholics and others recognize as the "natural law."[28] Natural
law, by definition, makes its claim upon all morally serious
human beings, regardless of their social status, cultural background, or religious loyalty. Its basic insights are open to all

through moral reasoning; though it may be clarified by specific divine revelations, like the Bible, its source is human nature itself understood from a moral point of view. Murray and countless Catholic moralists after him have emphasized the "dynamic" character of natural law, that is, its openness to development in light of historical experience.

Murray's dynamic conception of natural law, clearly, is the bishops' own. For their example of a "universal moral principle" is "non-combatant immunity,"[29] a norm that has been generally recognized, if not generally observed, only since the relatively recent professionalization of warfare in Western civilization. To propose "non-combatant immunity" as a universal moral principle is to claim that this principle, whatever its cultural antecedents, could and should become the object of a true consensus among all human beings willing to consider the problem of warfare from a moral point of view. The existence of such "universal moral principles," of course, lies at the basis of the pastoral letter's moral claim not just upon Catholics but upon all persons in a pluralistic society.[30] When, for example, the peace pastoral exhorts the nation to respect the principle of non-combatant immunity, its argument is addressed explicitly to all morally serious citizens and not just to Catholics.

Given this "natural law" understanding of universal moral principles, the bishops' conception of "formal Church teaching" fulfills a number of complex functions in moral reasoning specifically addressed to Catholics. As an interpretation of whatever moral agenda is to be discovered in divine revelation, "formal Church teaching" cannot help but determine the boundaries between the church as a community of moral discourse and the larger civil community in a pluralistic society. Loyalty to formal Church teaching, in short, is a condition for membership in the church as a community of moral discourse. This does not mean that anything labeled "formal Church teaching" requires blind obedience; if the church is a community of moral discourse, then, according to the pastoral letters, the appropriate response is to acknowledge such teaching as the premise for further dialogue defining religious praxis within the church.

As one would hope, considerable overlap exists between universal moral principles and formal Church teaching. Since God is One, both Creator and Redeemer, in principle there can be no conflict between the two. Nevertheless, they differ in that the former appeal to reason as embodied in the wisdom of human civilization as a whole, and the latter to faith as demonstrated in the believer's loyalty to the church. The history of Catholic social teaching shows, for example, that natural law arguments favoring the principle of "non-combatant immunity" were strengthened significantly by the concerns of Christian churches for the suffering of innocent persons. Conversely, the most prominent piece of formal Church teaching in "The Challenge of Peace," Vatican II's absolute condemnation of "total war," is justified by appeal to the principle of non-combatant immunity.[31] Formal Church teaching, therefore, is both a distillation from the continuing process of consensus formation within the community of moral discourse and an agenda for further reflection within it. I will try to clarify its role in setting the community's agenda for religious praxis and ethical reflection after introducing the third element, "prudential judgments."

Neither universal moral principles nor formal Church teaching, no matter how vividly they are presented, as yet provide either a concrete policy recommendation or an all-things-considered judgment on how in a particular set of circumstances these principles are to be applied. A careful analysis of the logic of moral reasoning, in any community of moral discourse, indicates that there is an important step between, for example, the condemnation of "total war" and the advocacy of a policy of "no first use" of nuclear weapons, that itself must be scrutinized in public dialogue. Informed by the traditionally Catholic view of the decisive role of the virtue of "prudence" in moral reasoning, the bishops refer to this step as "prudential judgment." What they have in mind is clearly not the amoral calculations that typically confuse prudence with instrumental reason as such, but the habitual exercise of moral discernment by which the significance of particular circumstances is allowed to shape the interpretive application of moral principles.[32] Thoughtful persons, even though loyal to each other in the same community of moral discourse, as likely as not will arrive at differing prudential judgments, because moral discernment is itself a manifestation of personal character and not simply a calculus based strictly on the facts of the case.

Thus, for example, the bishops' advocacy of a policy of "no first use" is not strictly entailed by their adherence to Vatican II's absolute condemnation of "total war." To advocate a "no first use" of nuclear weapons is to enter into a complex policy debate involving, among other things, the history of the so-called "Cold War" in Europe, the current defense posture of NATO, the controllability of nuclear exchanges once initiated by either side, the impact of such a declaration on the political morale of friend and foe alike, and the plausibility of non-nuclear deterrence strategies.[33] Each of these issues, of course, involves technical questions, about which even experts disagree in good faith. But over and above such disagreements regarding the "facts," to say that "no first use" is based on prudential judgments is to imply that a certain moral discernment, ultimately a reflection on the character of those discerning it, is leading the bishops to envision one sort of future for the planet as opposed to another, and to accept one set of risks, rather than another, in getting there.

Needless to say, lack of consensus over prudential judgments is to be expected in any community of moral discourse, whatever its size and structure. That being the case, aren't Michael Novak and the lay commissions right in reserving prudential judgments to the laity's individual consciences? Don't the bishops violate the formal norms for any community of moral discourse if they insist on teaching their own prudential judgments? The answer depends on what the bishops hope to accomplish by such teaching. If the bishops intend to foreclose further discussion by presenting their prudential judgments as, without further ado, binding upon the consciences of the participants within the community, they would violate the norms of communicative competence which govern even their vocation as Christian moral teachers. If, on the other hand, they intend only to stimulate further discussion by showing as concretely as possible what they believe it would mean to practice what they preach, they would not violate these norms. For by presenting their prudential judgments precisely as prudential judgments, they are asserting their own commitment to an open-ended process of dialogue inevitably ruled by "the peculiarly forceless force of better arguments."

As careful analysis of the third and final drafts of "The Challenge of Peace" and the first three drafts of the pastoral letter on the economy clearly shows, the bishops have presented their prudential judgments as such and have asked only that they "be given serious attention and consideration by Catholics as they determine whether their moral judgments are consistent with the Gospel."[34] While others may find their conclusions congenial, depending upon reasons not necessarily grounded in the bishops' own distinctive patterns of discernment, Catholics are asked only to acknowledge the religious competence of their teachers and thus make themselves accountable to them in public dialogue. They are neither forced to accept nor free to ignore the bishops' conclusions, but invited, if they do dissent on prudential grounds, to contribute a more discerning reading of the principles they share with the bishops.

Indeed, the final draft of "The Challenge of Peace" not only structures its arguments in terms of this threefold distinction of levels of moral teaching, but also calls for the development of a pedagogy consistent with it. Citing "the Church's obligation to provide its members with the help they need in forming their consciences," the bishops invite the whole "civil community" to participate in the process of learning to make "correct and responsible moral judgments."[35] Here is the letter's pedagogical proposal:

> The Church's educational programs must explain clearly those principles or teachings about which there is little question. Those teachings which seek to make explicit the gospel call to peace and the traditions of the Church, should then be applied to concrete situations. They must indicate what the possible legitimate options are and what the consequences of those options may be. While this approach should be self-evident, it needs to be emphasized. Some people who have entered the public debate on nuclear warfare, at all points on the spectrum of opinion, appear not to understand or accept some of the clear teachings of the Church as contained in papal or conciliar documents. For example, some would place almost no limits on the use of nuclear weapons if they are needed for "self-defense." Some on the other side of the debate insist on conclusions which may be legitimate options but cannot be made obligatory on the basis of actual Church teaching.[36]

In order to overcome the confusion created by enthusiasts of either stripe, the church's programs of moral education ought to be consistent with the threefold distinction. In order to understand the force of the bishops' criticism of the policy debate among Catholics, however, we need now to focus more specifically on the role of "formal Church teaching" in framing public policy discussion.

Because the role of "formal Church teaching" in such policy discussion is similar for all Christian communities seeking to build, in H. Richard Niebuhr's words, the "kingdom on earth," it is useful to take our cue from American Protestant traditions of ethical reflection. In particular, the so-called "middle axioms" approach appears very illuminating here.[37] As formulated by J. H. Oldham and John C. Bennett, middle axioms bridge the gap between "guiding principles about which there could be no disagreement" and support of admittedly controversial public policies.[38] Mediating between the two, middle axioms were "to define the directions which, in a particular state of society, Christian faith must express itself."[39] Their best analogue in Catholic tradition is the effort inspired by Vatican II's *Gaudium et Spes* to "scrutiniz[e] . . . the signs of the times," to which we shall return in chapter six. While most of the Protestant discussion of middle axioms has centered on their logical status, new ground can be broken by analyzing how middle axioms actually help create a community of moral discourse, in light of Habermas' normative view of "truth-dependent mode(s) of socialization." In *Polity and Praxis* Strain and I argued that middle axioms formulate the community's "generalizable interests" for public dialogue in a pluralistic society.

To formulate a "generalizable interest," a community of moral discourse must have reached or be hoping to reach consensus on two major points: (1) The public policy guideline being proposed must be an *authentic* reflection of the community's own particular tradition of moral discernment, and once recognized as such by members of the community it serves as the focal point for their contribution to public dialogue. (2) At the same time, the policy guideline must be regarded as *appropriate* to society as a whole, in the sense that it could and should become the basis for consensus, not just within the religious community but also within the civil community as a whole.[40] Thus a generalizable interest is, in Habermas's words, "the *common* interest ascertained *without deception*": it defines the particular community's authentic sense of the public good to be pursued in common with all other communities in society.[41] Given the complex requirements involved in making this twofold claim for consensus, any middle axiom proposed within the church as a community of moral discourse will necessarily, like Janus, address two audiences simultaneously: both the church as a particular community of moral discourse and the larger civil community in a pluralistic society. While by now it should be obvious that the pastoral letters generally exhibit this Janus-faced character, the role of "formal Church teaching" in setting the direction of the claims toward either audience must still be made explicit.

By couching their argument in the idiom of formal Church teaching, the bishops thus are not pre-empting discussion among either Catholics or their fellow citizens. Instead, fully consistent with their religious competence as Catholic bishops, they are proposing an agenda for the community's public dialogue, based on their reading of the signs of the times. They are not simply rehearsing the commonplaces of the tradition they share with other members of the Catholic community; much less are they giving a short course for the public at large in the history of Catholic social teaching. Their point is to allow this tradition to define a practical perspective on the concrete historical moment being faced, not only by the community but also by society as a whole. This exercise in discernment, of course, is always geared to the needs of praxis, both religious and social. Hence, what results is not simply another theoretical speculation, but a concrete action-guideline that translates the bishops' sense of the tradition and its proposed claims upon its twofold audience. Formal Church teaching must yield a middle axiom, then, that mediates between relatively abstract "universal moral principles" and quite specific "prudential judgments" involved in recommending actual policies. It goes without saying that the discussion of both the middle axioms and the formal Church teaching warranting them must proceed within the general rules of communicative competence. For presumably the bishops do intend to foster a genuine consensus, the formation of which must be determined by "the peculiarly forceless force of better arguments."

Let me illustrate the agenda-setting role played by "formal Church teaching" by examining the controversial "option for the poor" featured prominently in all three drafts of the pastoral letter on the economy. Though they are in substantial agreement with the first draft, I will confine my remarks to the second and third drafts, which more clearly illustrate the complexity involved in proposing an option for the poor, or any other theme, as a middle axiom. First of all, there is no doubt that the option for the poor makes its claim as neither a "universal moral principle" nor a "prudential judgment." It is introduced toward the end of the section on "The Christian Vision of Economic Life," and there the arguments for it are intrinsically theological and warranted by the particular tradition of religious praxis informing the Catholic community of moral discourse.[42] Yet its purpose is not just to dramatize the meaning of that tradition for the community, but to establish "moral priorities for the nation." After recognizing the perennial need to protect everyone's human rights implicit in the universal moral principle of "justice for all," the bishops thus return to the option for the poor in order to clarify their demand that "the poor have the single most urgent claim on the conscience of the nation."[43] Indeed, they take pains to defend the option for the poor as a truly generalizable interest: "Not an adversarial slogan which pits one group or class against another . . . , it states that the deprivation and powerlessness of the poor wounds the whole community."[44] They claim, in other words, that it is "the *common* interest ascertained *without deception*." The bishops then outline three policy priorities implicit in the option, culminating in a commitment to the "New American Experiment in Democracy." Yet the option itself, of course, is not a policy recommendation. As this analysis suggests, "prudential judgments" must still be made in order to determine which policies would be consistent with the option for the poor, and which not.

If the option for the poor defines the agenda implicit in "formal Church teaching," what is its authority within the Catholic community of moral discourse? Is it part of the pervasive reality of "selective Catholicism" or does it define some sort of moral absolute in Catholic social teaching? The "option" language itself is relatively new and controversial. The Latin American bishops' conference, meeting at Puebla, Mexico in 1979, officially endorsed a "preferential option for the poor,"[45] and language similar to theirs can be found in the statements of Popes Paul VI and John Paul II.[46] Nevertheless, the formula has also been criticized by those who identify it with certain Marxist-Leninist interpretations of Latin American liberation theology.[47] Responsive to the concerns of both the advocates and the critics of the Latin American "option," the drafting committee has attempted to do two possibly incompatible things simultaneously: to show solidarity with the Latin American bishops' conference by adopting their formula, but also to signal their reservations about liberation theology by refusing to interpret it as an "adversarial slogan." This deft maneuver the pastoral letter's second and third drafts accomplish, not just by dropping the term "preferential," but also by explicitly recognizing the "common good" understood as "justice for all" as the appropriate context in which to affirm the option itself.

It is encouraging to note that Michael Novak, a formidable opponent of the model of political economy usually operative in Latin American liberation theology,[48] in his recent work, *Freedom with Justice*, has admitted that "the 'option for the poor' is the correct option."[49] Though he then goes on to identify that option with public policies favoring "private ownership, . . . incentives, and . . . markets," it would be naive to think that Novak's endorsement of the option is simply a ploy to keep his critics off balance. I prefer to think that, here at least, he is playing by the rules governing the church as a community of moral discourse. He seems to be conceding that the bishops have formulated a truly generalizable interest, and that the really crucial arguments about it will concern which sets of prudential judgments are used to spell out its concrete meaning for public policy. Viewed in that light, the option for the poor is neither an absolute in the traditional sense, nor another fragment of "selective Catholicism." As arguably "the *common* interest ascertained *without deception*," it bears the promise of the church's struggle to seek consensus through public dialogue. By giving it the serious attention that it deserves, American Catholics are reconstituting themselves as a community of moral discourse.

Despite this noteworthy advance in the direction of public dialogue, not all problems implicit in the pastoral letters' complex structure of moral authority have been resolved. Let me conclude this chapter by citing two of these problems, both of them with practical as well as theoretical dimensions. The first of these is illustrated by the conference at Notre Dame, previously discussed in chapter two, and concerns the ambiguous role of competence in public argument. That ambiguity arises from the tension between the kind of utopianly unrestricted participation called for by Habermas and Gustafson, and the kind of realistic appreciation for the contributions of recognized achievement that Andrew Greeley advocated in his criticism of the "Call to Action" process. The tension, in turn, reflects the difficulty in any self-governing association of reconciling the demand for inclusive participation of all interested parties with the equally stringent demands that such association makes upon specialized expertise. There are possible trade-offs, in other words, between the ideal of a generalized communicative competence and the realities imposed by a recognition of religious and professional competence.

Even in an "ideal speech situation" where only "the peculiarly forceless force of better arguments" prevails, the participation of those most affected by these arguments eventually will tend to become peripheral because of their likely incompetence in judging complex policy questions. At Notre Dame, for example, some of the participants spoke eloquently on behalf of the poor and the unemployed; but none of them were themselves poor and unemployed. Representatives of these "marginalized" groups, of course, were not excluded from the hearing at Notre Dame; but neither were they specifically invited. Instead, the participants in the symposium were people with impeccable credentials, and the quality of their interaction generally reflected the kind of mutual respect that experts tender to one another, even in their disagreements. The question raised in construing that conference as a model of public dialogue is, of course, to what extent the participation of "marginalized" groups is necessary if Catholic religious praxis is to proceed according to the norms of communicative competence, especially in the church's proposed "New Experiment in Democracy."

There is no straightforward answer to this question. I can only second Gustafson's practical advice that in a community of moral discourse, religious leaders must specifically ensure that no members are excluded from the group's deliberations. Habermas's theory of "truth-dependent mode(s) of socialization" addresses this question only peripherally, asserting, in effect, that participants, however lacking in either professional or religious competencies can only marginalize themselves by demonstrating their own complicity in "systematically distorted communication." Habermas does not address the tensions likely to arise between communicative, professional, and religious competence, either because his is a utopian faith in dialogue, or because his theory tacitly addresses itself exclusively to an idealized "civil community," and not to the concrete communities in which real people with radically differing interests, cultures, and personal capabilities actually dwell, or possibly because of some combination of both reasons. Rather than speculate on the shape of the theoretical *tour de force* required to overcome this ambiguity, let me merely suggest that the success of the bishops' "New Experiment in Democracy" will depend on how well the church faces up to the trade-offs involved in committing itself to a truly participatory model of consensus formation. Though these are real, they cannot fully be understood, let alone dealt with, apart from still further experiment seeking to democratize the religious praxis of the church.

The second problem involved in using the pastoral letters' complex structure of moral authority as a model for the church as a community of moral discourse, is that it places the bishops under a certain burden of proof regarding the way in which they approach issues in any other area of Catholic moral teaching. If it is possible to consult not just Catholic clergy and laity but also the American "civil community" as a whole, when reformulating Catholic social teaching on nuclear deterrence and U.S. employment policies, why can't a similar process be used to respond to the current *sensus fidelium* on a host of other sensitive issues like birth control, abortion, divorce, sexual ethics in general, and the role of women in the church in particular? Catholic theologian Daniel Maguire correctly posed the problem when he asked why the bishops couldn't extend the same kind of nuanced sympathy to women facing unwanted pregnancies that "The Challenge of Peace" shows to U.S. military personnel operating the nation's missile silos.[50] Ultimately, the same problem of moral consistency is posed by the American bishops' apparent acquiescence in the Vatican's silencing of Charles E. Curran at Catholic University in Washington.

Judging from the vicissitudes of the bishops' proposed pastoral letter on the role of women in the church, the burden of living up consistently to the standards of moral discourse implicit in the letters on nuclear deterrence and the economy may not be discharged successfully by the bishops, unless the Catholic laity and interested parties in the larger "civil community" continue to assert themselves on these sensitive issues. Indeed the letter on the role of women may already have been hopelessly compromised with the forced resignation of certain members of the drafting committee's staff, on the grounds that they had already publicly advocated controversial positions in advance of the bishops' teaching. If public silence on controversial issues is a condition for participation in the drafting process, then by rights neither Brian Hehir nor George G. Higgins should have been asked to advise the bishops on the previous pastoral letters. Of course, given the professional achievements of these two outspoken priests who epitomize so well the aspirations of both the old and the newer Catholic social activism, it would have been unthinkable to exclude either one of them. It should be equally unthinkable to request the resignations of outspoken women with equally impressive credentials.

At this point we simply cannot know how severe these problems actually may turn out to be. Only in the context of a serious effort to keep the public dialogue going within the church, will it become apparent whether these problems are the predictable kinks accompanying any new learning process, or a cancer that will surely kill the "New American Experiment in Democracy." In view of these problems, we can say no more than that the pastoral letter process is a promising point of departure for elaborating a consensual theory of truth in Catholic moral teaching. When interpreted in the context of Catholicism's own traditions of "civility" and "truthfulness," and of a normative view of human association that highlights the "communicative competence" presupposed by any successful human interaction, as we have seen in this chapter, the pastoral letters' threefold structure of authoritative teaching does provide a magna charta for legitimate dissent within the church. And unless the church establishes some such ground rules for dissent, it has no basis for claiming to represent a genuine moral consensus. The expectations raised by the pastoral letter process, however, will not be realized unless the church seizes this opportunity and strives to become a genuine community of moral discourse. Only then will Catholicism be able to transform the pastoral letters' promising new beginning into an enduring contribution to the building of the Kingdom of God in America.

Notes

1. H. Richard Niebuhr, *The Kingdom of God in America* (New York: Harper and Row, 1959).

2. *Ibid.*, p. ix.

3. *Ibid.*, p. xii.

4. *Ibid.*, p. x.

5. James M. Gustafson, "The Church: A Community of Moral Discourse," in *The Church as Moral Decision-Maker* (Philadelphia: Pilgrim Press, 1970), pp. 83-95.

6. *Ibid.*, p. 84.

7. *Ibid.*, p. 86.

8. *Ibid.*

9. *Ibid.*, p. 88.

10. *Ibid.*, p. 90.

11. *Ibid.*, p. 95.

12. *Ibid.*, pp. 93-4.

13. Hans Küng, *Truthfulness: The Future of the Church* (London: Sheed and Ward, 1968), p. 62.

14. Jürgen Habermas, *Legitimation Crisis* (Boston: Beacon Press, 1975), p. 142; cf. Dennis P. McCann and Charles R. Strain, *Polity and Praxis: A Program for American Practical Theology* (Minneapolis, Minnesota: Winston Press/Seabury Books, 1985), pp. 38-64, 152-61.

15. Jürgen Habermas, *The Theory of Communicative Action. Volume One: Reason and the Rationalization of Society* (Boston: Beacon Press, 1984), p. 278.

16. McCann and Strain, *op. cit.*, p. 52-7.

17. Cf. Jürgen Habermas, "Vorbereitende Bemerkungen zu einer Theorie der kommunikativen Kompetenz," in *Theorie der Gesellschaft oder Sozialtechnologie: Was leistet die Systemforschung?* (Frankfurt am Main: Suhrkamp, 1971), pp. 101-41; Habermas, "Die Universalitaetsanspruch der Hermeneutik," in *Hermeneutik und Ideologiekritik* (Frankfurt am Main: Suhrkamp, 1971), pp. 120-59); Habermas, *Communication and the Evolution of Society* (Boston: Beacon Press, 1979); and Habermas, *The Theory of Communicative Action*. Volume One, pp. 1-42, 75-101, 273-337; cf. Dennis P. McCann, "Habermas and the Theologians," in *Religious Studies Review*, Vol. 7, No. 1 (January, 1981), pp. 14-21.

18. Habermas, "Vorbereitende Bemerkungen zu einer Theorie der kommunikativen Kompetenz," p. 137.

19. Though a capacity for ideological self-criticism may be implicit in the very notion of public dialogue, skeptics have good reasons to doubt that Catholic social teaching is capable of such self-criticism. Evidence to the contrary would have to include Charles E. Curran's groundbreaking study, *Directions in Catholic Social Ethics* (Notre Dame, Indiana: University of Notre Dame Press, 1985).

20. Cf. John Courtney Murray, *We Hold These Truths: Catholic Reflections on the American Proposition* (Garden.City, New York: Doubleday Image Books, 1964), pp. 112, 280-317.

21. James Castelli, *The Bishops and the Bomb: Waging Peace in a Nuclear Age* (Garden City, New York: Doubleday Image Books, 1983), p. 93.

22. Philip Lawler, *How Bishops Decide: An American Catholic Case Study* (Washington, D.C.: Ethics and Public Policy Center, 1986), p. 24.

23. The format of the University of Santa Clara Conference on the First Draft of "Catholic Social Teaching and the U.S. Economy," sponsored by the Institute on Poverty and Conscience, January 25-7, 1985, at the University of Santa Clara in California, suggests that the quality of the public dialogue achieved at the Notre Dame conference was not a flash in the pan.

24. Cf. John W. Houck and Oliver F. Williams, eds., *Catholic Social Teaching and the U.S. Economy: Working Papers for a Bishops' Pastoral* (Washington, D.C.: University Press of America, 1984), pp. 23-138.

25. Rev. Jan Schotte's memorandum was published as "A Vatican Synthesis" in *Origins* (April 7, 1983), pp. 690-695; cf. Castelli, *op. cit.*, pp. 138-48, for an account of the leak and its impact.

26. National Conference of Catholic Bishops, *The Challenge of Peace: God's Promise and Our Response* (Washington, D.C.: United States Catholic Conference, 1983), par. 9-10.

27. *Pastoral Constitution on the Church in the Modern World (Gaudium et Spes)*, par. 43, in Walter M. Abbott, ed., *The Documents of Vatican II* (London: Geoffrey Chapman, 1967), p. 244.

28. Cf. Josef Fuchs, S.J., *Natural Law: A Theological Investigation* (New York: Sheed and Ward, 1965); and James M. Gustafson, *Protestant and Roman Catholic Ethics: Prospects for Rapprochement* (Chicago: University of Chicago Press, 1978), pp. 80-94.

29. National Conference of Catholic Bishops, *The Challenge of Peace*, par. 9.

30. *Ibid.*, par. 17.

31. *Ibid.*, par. 147-9.

32. Cf. James M. Gustafson, "Moral Discernment in the Christian Life," in *Theology and Christian Ethics* (Philadelphia: Pilgrim Press, 1974), pp. 99-119, esp. pp. 118-9.

33. Cf. McGeorge Bundy, Morton H. Halperin, William W. Kaufmann, George F. Kennan, Robert S. McNamara, Madalene O'Donnell, Leon V. Sigal, Gerard C. Smith, Richard H. Ullman, Paul C. Warnke, "Back from the brink: The case for a new U.S. nuclear strategy," in *The Atlantic Monthly*, Vol. 258, No. 2 (August 1986), pp. 35-41.

34. National Conference of Catholic Bishops, *op. cit.*, par. 10.

35. *Ibid.*, par. 281.

36. *Ibid.*, par. 283.

37. McCann and Strain, *op. cit.*, pp. 152-69; cf. Dennis P. McCann, "A Second Look at Middle Axioms," in *The Annual of the Society of Christian Ethics*, 1981, pp. 73-96.

38. John C. Bennett, *Christian Ethics and Social Policy* (New York: Charles Scribner's Sons, 1946), p. 79.

39. J. H. Oldham, "The Function of the Church in Society," in W. A. Visser 'T Hooft and J. H. Oldham, *The Church and its Function in Society* (Chicago: Willett, Clark and Company, 1937), pp. 91-238.

40. Murray, *op. cit*, pp. 86-125.

41. Habermas, *Legitimation Crisis*, p. 108; cf. Dennis P. McCann, "The Good to be Pursued in Common" (Unpublished paper given at the symposium on "Catholic Social Teaching and the Common Good," sponsored by the University of Notre Dame's Center for Ethics and Religious Values in Business, held April 14-16, 1986).

42. National Conference of Catholic Bishops, *The Second Draft: Catholic Social Teaching and the U.S. Economy*, in *Origins*, Vol. 15, No. 17 (October 10, 1985), par. 59; *The Third Draft: Economic Justice for All: Catholic Social Teaching and the U.S. Economy*, in *Origins*, Vol. 16, No. 3 (June 5, 1986), par. 52.

43. National Conference of Catholic Bishops, *The Second Draft*, par. 88; *The Third Draft*, par. 85.

44. National Conference of Catholic Bishops, *The Second Draft*, par. 90; *The Third Draft*, par. 87.

45. Cf. "The Puebla Final Document," in John Eagleson and Philip Scharper, eds., *Puebla and Beyond* (Maryknoll, New York: Orbis Books, 1979), pp. 264-7.

46. Cf. National Conference of Catholic Bishops, *The Second Draft*, par. 89; *The Third Draft*, par. 86.

47. Cf. Cardinal Joseph Ratzinger, "Instructions on certain aspects of the theology of liberation," in the *National Catholic Reporter* (September 21, 1984), pp. 11-4, which reaffirms the "option for the poor" but forbids using it as a pretext for developing a Marxist-Leninist interpretation of the Gospel.

48. Cf. Michael Novak, *The Spirit of Democratic Capitalism* (New York: American Enterprise Institute/Simon and Schuster, 1982), pp. 287-97ff; cf. Michael Novak, ed., *Liberation South, Liberation North* (Washington, D.C.: American Enterprise Institute, 1981); for an attempt to criticize liberation theology on the basis of theological criteria implicit in liberation theology itself, cf. McCann, *Christian Realism and Liberation Theology: Practical Theologies in Creative Conflict* (Maryknoll, New York: Orbis Books, 1981), pp. 156-233.

49. Michael Novak, *Freedom with Justice: Catholic Social Thought and Liberal Institutions* (San Francisco: Harper and Row, 1984), p. 192.

50. Cf. Daniel Maguire, "Abortion: A Question of Catholic Honesty," in *The Christian Century*, Vol. 100, No. 26 (September 14-21, 1983), pp. 803-7.

5

JUSTICE AS PARTICIPATION: AN AMERICANIST PRACTICAL THEOLOGY

In the eucharist Christians from every walk of life gather as members of a people baptized into Christ's death and resurrection. They hear the Word of God proclaimed: a word of hope for the poor and the oppressed, a call to accountability for those more powerful and more fortunate. The community asks the Holy Spirit to unite all present into the one living body of Christ. The one bread, one body, and one Spirit make the Christian community a sacrament or visible sign of the unity in justice and peace that God wills for the whole of humanity. For this community to be an effective sign to the world, it must ceaselessly pursue an end to divisions in its own life and the life of society.

— Paragraph 64, "Catholic Social Teaching and the U.S. Economy: The Second Draft"

This nation's original experiment in democracy, historians tell us, was itself at least partially inspired by the development of Christianity in America. Fueled by the aspirations of dissenting religious communities, including recusant English Catholics, a common religious praxis emerged, one which eventually came to accept a plurality of responses to the call of building the Kingdom of God in America. The theology that interpreted this common American religious praxis has had its vicissitudes: while it clearly encouraged the prophetic Christianity of the Abolitionists, the recent civil rights movements, and the Protestant social gospel, it also justified Nativism, Prohibition, and various forms of imperialism under our common faith in America's Manifest Destiny. The Americanist tradition beginning with Isaac Hecker, far from encouraging the false disdain with which some Catholics have greeted these vicissitudes, has consciously identified with this common religious praxis and has tried to show how a mature American Catholicism might make a distinctive contribution to it.

In seeking to understand the movement toward the Kingdom of God in America, mainstream Protestant theology has attached great significance to God's special Providence in history. Typically commencing with echoes of John Winthrop's sermon to the Puritans about to disembark at Plymouth Rock, this theology affirms not just a covenant between God and the new Americans, but also the possibility of a special role for it in the world's historic movement toward the Kingdom: "For wee must Consider that wee shall be as a Citty vpon a Hill, the eies of all people are vppon vs; . . . " Americanist Catholics, however, have transformed this shared theological assumption regarding God's special Providence in light of the distinctively Catholic vision of God, its Trinitarian perspective on the nature of the Divine Life, and the role of the Christian community within that Life. Beginning with Hecker, Americanist Catholics have posed the Trinitarian vision of God, not as an alternative to the building of the kingdom on earth, but as the most illuminating model for it. The indwelling of the Holy Spirit, in individuals as well as in communities, is for them the key to understanding the dynamism of God's movement through history.

Though this same Trinitarian vision of God also informs the tradition of Catholic social teaching discussed in the N.C.C.B.'s recent pastoral letters, Catholic social teaching as interpreted in this country remains remarkably inattentive to its own inner connection with our common American religious praxis. Yet, as I will argue in the next chapter, the letters' "New American Ex-

periment in Democracy" is best understood as a Catholic contribution to this common praxis of building the kingdom on
earth. As such the "New Experiment" is predicated upon an improbable theological synthesis of two elements that H.
Richard Niebuhr saw mostly in contrast: Catholic contemplation of the
Divine Life (*visio Dei*) and Protestant action in response to the
movement of that Life in history (*regnum Dei*).[1] The synthesis
of the two operative in the "New Experiment in Democracy,"
cannot be fully appreciated apart from an Americanist interpretation of the Trinitarian vision of God, which in this chapter I
hope to provide as a basis for understanding the pastoral letters'
view of social justice as participation.

A suitable place to begin explaining how the Trinitarian
vision of God inspires a distinctively Catholic contribution to
building the kingdom on earth is provided, appropriately
enough, by Methodist theologian Larry Rasmussen. In one of
the most theologically provocative critiques of the first draft of
the pastoral letter on the U.S. economy, Rasmussen challenged
the N.C.C.B. to ground its hesitant call for the "New Experiment" in a theology flavored more robustly with the biblical legacy of "the Exodus-Sinai event."[2] Two conflicting "half-formed
paradigms" govern the theology and, hence, the policy recommendations of the letter: one, "A New Experiment in Economic
Democracy," which seeks to empower the poor in fidelity to "the
dangerous memory" of Exodus-Sinai; the other, "Son of New
Deal," which would reconcile both the rich and the poor along
lines ultimately traceable to the ideology and institutions of the
Israelite monarchy. While both paradigms are "authentically
Biblical," Rasmussen insists that only the Exodus-Sinai event
can be taken as "constitutive of Jewish and Christian faith."
Nevertheless, because the bishops have been unable to establish truly biblical priorities between the two paradigms, their
policy recommendations for the "New American Experiment,"
especially their strategies for empowering the poor, seem curiously half-hearted.

While I share some of Rasmussen's reservations about the
letter's recommendations, his view of the conflicting theological
paradigms is not ultimately persuasive. Contrary to Rasmussen, I see but one paradigm emerging in the pastoral letters'
theology, a paradigm of social transformation rooted not directly in any particular biblical legacy, but in the Trinitarian
vision of God traditional to Catholic faith. Rasmussen himself
almost glimpses this perspective, at least in its practical implications, but just as quickly dismisses these as "the long Constantinian hangover that wants everyone on board dialoguing,
especially the influence wielders." The "long Constantinian
hangover," of course, refers to traditional Catholic religious
praxis, whose ideal of public dialogue has so often been corrupted into an instrument of domination, clerical and otherwise. Nevertheless, the half-heartedness that Rasmussen
rightly denounces is due not to a conflict between two
paradigms, but to a failure to follow through on the promise of
the one operative in the letter: the Trinitarian vision of God.
Properly understood, this paradigm suggests that the poor can
truly be empowered only in a dialogue that includes everyone,
even "the influence wielders," not just in society but also in the
church. For it alone discloses the ultimate, and hence incorrup-
tible, pattern of justice as participation.

A satisfactory argument in response to Rasmussen's challenge must begin, I think, with a reminder about the traditional
Catholic attitude toward the Bible. Catholicism recognizes no
canon within the canon of Scriptures apart from the revelation
of God in Jesus Christ. Furthermore, this revelation itself is not
exhausted in the Scriptures, but is also to be discovered in
Christian traditions that can claim to derive from the teachings
of Jesus' apostles. Indeed, the church itself is the living interpre-
ter of both the Scriptures and traditions, in virtue of Jesus'
promised gift of the Holy Spirit.[3] These assertions mean that
from a Catholic perspective neither the Exodus-Sinai event nor
the Israelite monarchy is "constitutive of Jewish and Christian
faith." What is constitutive is the unceasing activity of the Holy

Spirit interpreting the revelation of Jesus Christ within authentically Christian communities of faith.

Rasmussen to the contrary notwithstanding, the admittedly diverse biblical legacies cannot be played off against each other when it comes to discerning the will of the Holy Spirit for these communities today. Nor can they, either singly or collectively, be used to dismiss the greater part of the Catholic community's own historic experience as a "long Constantinian hangover." However inadequate the theology and institutions characteristic of the Constantinian period may be for our purposes, they, too, continue to make a contribution, despite their corruption, to the work of the Holy Spirit in history. But to convince you that this rejoinder to Rasmussen's Protestant perspective is anything more than Catholic special pleading on behalf of "the influence wielders," let me reconstruct, at least in outline, the Trinitarian vision of God and suggest how it actually governs both the theology and the policy recommendations of the pastoral letters. My sketch, of course, will be deliberately Americanist; for unless the letters' theology is given an Americanist interpretation, Rasmussen's analysis seems unanswerable.

An Americanist understanding of the Trinitarian vision of God is distinctive for its acute sensitivity to the historic moment. A departure from traditional Catholic emphasis upon the "perennial" truth of orthodox formulas like the Nicene Creed, an authentically Americanist perspective strives to be a living response to the manner of God's presence in history, particular to this place at this time in this particular culture. An Americanist response to the Trinitarian vision of God, therefore, is inconceivable apart from a special discernment of what Vatican II called "the signs of the times." Isaac Hecker's own spiritual pilgrimage before the Civil War, as he moved toward conversion to Catholicism, provides a key illustration of the role that such discernment plays in this perspective on the Trinity. Hecker became a Catholic when he realized, as you will recall from chapter one, that his own experience only made sense in terms of the active

presence of the Holy Spirit within both the church and society
as a whole.

To be sure, Hecker was a "religious virtuoso," one of those
rare persons whose spiritual dispositions are self-authenticat-
ing and not the conventional results of a pious upbringing.[4]
Though from a very early age possessed of an uncanny sense of
his own spiritual destiny, he was unsure of how that destiny
might be fulfilled. His restless experiments as a young man with
various forms of radical politics and utopian religious community, he later regarded as premature. Hecker became a Catholic
when he rather suddenly realized that the spirit governing his
life was none other than the Holy Spirit professed by Trinitarian
Christians. His conversion thus came not as a repudiation of his
Transcendentalist yearnings but as their fulfillment. Frus-
trated by the apparent arbitrariness of his own experimenting,
he now found relief in the conviction that the church, in principle, was the community in which the Holy Spirit's presence
could most fully be experienced. He could submit to its disci-
plines confident that the Spirit who prompted his own restless
enthusiasms was the same Spirit ordering and perfecting all
things, old and new, in the community.

Far from stifling his spiritual gifts, entry into the community permitted Hecker to expand his personal sense of destiny
into a truly seminal vision of the Catholic church's role in building the Kingdom of God in America. For the Spirit was leading
more than the soul of Isaac Hecker. The original American experiment in democracy, in Hecker's view, was itself a work of the
Holy Spirit, which through its constitutional separation of
church and state had emancipated both individuals and communities to make their own unique contributions to the history
of salvation. The Catholic church had to be the chief beneficiary
of the Spirit's work in America, for only the Catholic church possessed an ecclesiastical structure that, in the absence of government sponsorship, could order and perfect all the diverse enthusiasms that the Divine Life must engender in a free country.
Once purged of the routines of bureaucratic domination that

stemmed from the church's historic involvement with European states, the very structure of the Catholic community would manifest itself, not as a "Constantinian hangover," but as a unique contribution to the building of the Kingdom of God.

Any theological reflection consistent with Hecker's Americanist Catholicism, then, must become practical and historical. Since devotion to the Holy Spirit is not something peripheral to Catholic religious praxis, theological reflection upon it cannot take the form of an abstract pursuit of ultimate truth independent of its historic context, but must first of all become a critical response to the concrete history of a specific religious community. The Trinitarian vision of God, in short, cannot be fully understood apart from a living discernment of the workings of the Holy Spirit, shaping our destiny both as individuals and as an American people. While Hecker himself did not develop this practical theology, he clearly saw the vision and cultivated the religious praxis from which such an Americanist theology must follow.

When one turns from Hecker's Americanist perspective to the doctrines of traditional Trinitarian theology, the most promising point of convergence is the notion of divine "indwelling."[5] Fittingly described in the prayers of the church as the grace and peace of Christ and the fellowship of the Holy Spirit, the divine indwelling establishes a community of "mutual personal companionship" between God and the believer. Within this community, the divine conversation takes place by which the Trinity continually manifests itself. Yet this community between God and the believer is only a reflection of the perfect intercourse that constitutes the Divine Life within the Trinity itself. The eternal processions by which the Son is generated from the Father and the Holy Spirit is breathed forth from both of them, thus making the Divine Life itself the model, as well as the ultimate ground, for any community whatever. For the Trinitarian mystery can only be known at all in the diverse acts of self-communication by which the Divine Persons, Father, Son, and Holy Spirit, enliven the spirits of human persons and communities.

Thus, in this divine tautology, to know God is to participate in the community created by the Persons of the Trinity.

Trinitarian theology traditionally has attempted to grasp this mystery of the Divine Life as analogous to the dynamics of human understanding and love. The generation of the Son from the Father is like an utterance perfectly expressing a speaker's meaning. The Son thus is apprehended by believers as the Word of God. In mutually consenting to their love, the Father and the Son together breathe forth the Holy Spirit "as a loving embrace of the divine reality communicated."[6] The Holy Spirit thus is apprehended by believers as grace and freedom: "God within us as our anointing and sealing, our earnest of heaven, our guest, comforter and advocate, the interior call, . . . the stern adversary of the flesh, of sin, of legalism, the secret power of transformation within us that presses forward to the resurrection of the glorified body and the transfiguration of the world."[7] Clarified variously by these metaphors and analogies, Catholicism's constitutive experience of the divine indwelling has shaped decisively its basic ideal of human community, sacred and secular.

In outlining an Americanist understanding of this Trinitarian paradigm, I need not reconstruct all the details of traditional Catholic speculation upon the mystery of the Divine Life. Those just cited have been selected because they provide a link between the spiritual discernments of Isaac Hecker and the theology of the pastoral letters. Out of all the metaphors and analogies generated by the mystery of the divine indwelling, the root metaphor of "participation" best captures what Catholic religious praxis discovers at the heart of both secular and sacred communities. The experienced dynamism of the "Divine indwelling is such that the very being of God must be both social and egalitarian; hierarchical relations emerge only to mediate the difference between the being of God and all that is not God. Each of the three Persons of the Trinity shares in the Divine Life co-equally. There is no subordination or domination of one Person over the Others, based upon either ontological or historical considerations. Yet each participates in the self-communication of the Divine Life in a distinctive way, ways which expand the circle of participation to include the whole of God's creation. Catholic experience of the divine indwelling, in short, has tended to suggest a distinct model of communal participation, an ideal pattern of egalitarian and hierarchical relationships,[8] grounded in the Divine Life itself.

When such a model becomes a norm for human social organization, whether sacred or secular, human flourishing tends to appear in a distinctive pattern. Social relations become more highly valued than they are in philosophies of rugged individualism; and yet the self-realization of persons is not sacrificed to the exigencies of society as a whole. Personal existence remains incommunicably sacred, even though socialization is seen as the key to self-realization, and vice-versa. Just as in God all three Persons share equally in the mystery of the Divine Life, yet are individuated as Persons by dynamisms that are indispensable to their common Life as a whole; so in the ideal pattern of human flourishing all persons are equal in dignity, yet differentiated according to the manner of their participation in society as a whole, that is, according to their varying dispositions, needs, and contributions to the common good. While this pattern, so far, is admittedly nebulous, already it does rule out both anarchy and totalitarianism as incompatible with the dynamisms of the divine indwelling. Such is the lesson to be drawn from the church's ancient struggle to distinguish the Trinitarian vision of God from both "tritheism" and "modalism."[9]

Hierarchical forms of social organization, however, are not entirely ruled out; but they can only be justified by their functional contribution to the common good. Just as in God the Trinitarian pattern of plurality in unity provides devotees of each Person with no excuse for exclusivism or any other pattern of idolatry, so hierarchical office in any social organization should not be used to institutionalize the pretense of domination, patriarchal or otherwise. Catholicism's rejection of any subordinationist interpretation of the Trinitarian vision of God thus correlates well with placing the burden of proof upon any social theory or practice that departs from radical egalitarianism. Social differentiations, and the inequalities that inevitably follow from them, have no justification apart from their service to the common good, which is always already constituted by the flourishing of individual persons in community.

Catholic social teaching, as exhibited by the recent pastoral letters, has captured some, but not all, of the practical consequences of the Trinitarian vision of God. Thus when the second and third drafts of the letter on the economy describe the church's ideal of human community in terms of "solidarity," "participation," and "subsidiarity," they do so in ways that reflect the dynamism of the Trinity. Let us examine these three themes and then, from our Americanist perspective, zero in on the conclusions the pastoral letters have failed to draw from the Trinitarian paradigm.

"Love and solidarity," the first prerequisites for life in community, are presented explicitly as a reflection of the Divine Life in human history:

> Christians look forward in hope to a true communion among all persons with each other and with God. The Spirit of Christ labors in history to build up the bonds of solidarity among all persons until that day on which their union is brought to perfection in the Kingdom of God. Indeed Christian theological reflection on the very reality of God as a trinitarian unity of persons — Father, Son, and Holy Spirit — shows that being a person means being united to other persons in mutual love.[10]

Far from being the usual abstract exhortation to love, the letter's meditation on the Trinitarian vision of God concretely identifies solidarity as a work of the Holy Spirit in history: "Solidarity is another name for this social friendship and civic commitment that makes human moral and economic life possible." The paradigm for this "social friendship and civic commitment" in human forms of association is, of course, the community of Divine Persons in the Trinity.

Equally significant is the letter's linking of "basic justice" and "participation." As a theological metaphor "participation" describes the relationship of all created being toward God, insofar as the divine indwelling sustains all that is. Whatever is good, is good ultimately in virtue of its participation in the perfection of God, whose good is always already realized in the dynamic life of the Trinity. As a norm for social organization, however, "participation" symbolizes the ultimate meaning of "basic justice," insofar as human flourishing cannot be sustained without it:

> Stated positively, justice demands that social institutions be ordered in a way that guarantees all persons the ability to participate actively in the economic, political, and cultural life of society. The level of participation may legitimately be greater for some persons than for others, but there is a basic level of access that must be made available for all. Such participation is an essential expression of the social nature of human beings and of their communitarian vocation.[11]

As a social analogue to "the grace and peace of Jesus Christ and the fellowship of the Holy Spirit," justice empowers persons for participation in the life of the human community. Conversely, the injustice of "marginalization" occurs whenever persons are excluded from or denied "a basic level of access" to "the economic, political and cultural life of society." To be marginalized is to be deprived of the power, available only in "love and solidarity," to overcome one's alienation from the community, whatever its causes. The injustice involved in marginalization thus is akin to sin against the Holy Spirit.

The third element in Catholic social teaching reflecting the Trinitarian vision of God is the frequently misunderstood principle of "subsidiarity." First formulated in Pius XI's encyclical, *Quadragesimo anno* (1931), subsidiarity ostensibly sets certain limits to the role of government in the organization of society as a whole:

> Just as it is gravely wrong to take from individuals what they can accomplish by their own initiative and industry and give it to the community, so also it is an injustice and at the same time a grave evil and disturbance of right order to assign to a greater and higher association what lesser and subordinate organizations can do. For every social activity ought of its very nature to furnish help to the members of the body social, and never destroy and absorb them.[12]

The issue at stake in this principle can be appreciated by asking the right question, as Thomas F. Duffy once did: "In considering any two groups representing various levels of social organization, . . . which is subsidiary to which?"[13] Because no form of human association should usurp what "individuals . . . can accomplish by their own initiative and industry," the help given by "a greater and higher association" must be subsidiary to the so-called "lesser and subordinate organizations" and the individuals participating in them. No doubt, there's a certain irony involved in describing such organizations — including the church — as "subordinate." While Pope Pius XI may have intended this principle merely as a roadblock in the path of Fascist expansionism, the drafts of the pastoral letter on the economy use it in two different ways. On the one hand, it serves to defend governmental intervention when necessary for "protecting human rights and securing basic justice for all members of the commonwealth"[14] against libertarian theories of the minimal state. On the other hand, it is invoked to make a distinction between the kind of public "partnerships" that the bishops envision for the "New American Experiment in Democracy"[15] and the centralized economic planning still advocated by some socialists. Clearly the principle is of decisive importance for understanding the true bearing of Catholic social teaching.

Neither *Quadragesimo anno* nor the N.C.C.B. pastoral letters discuss the theological presuppositions of the principle of subsidiarity. But I would argue that it, just as crucially as the ideals of "solidarity" and "participation," must be interpreted in light of the Trinitarian vision. For the assumptions operative in the principle of subsidiarity mirror the complex integration of hierarchical and egalitarian dynamisms suggested by the theological metaphors describing the Divine Life. The principle of subsidiarity thus presupposes a certain form of egalitarianism: In recognizing the legitimate autonomy of individuals and "subordinate" forms of human association, it ascribes to each individual person a God-given dignity, including the right and the duty of each to have primary responsibility for his or her own destiny. Furthermore, though hierarchy is also presupposed in the use of terms like "higher" and "lesser," the very idea of "subsidiary function" suggests that there is only one justification for hierarchical institutions in any society, namely, to give assistance (*"subsidium"*) to persons and self-governing associations that actually need help in fulfilling their respective destinies. "He who would be master of all must first become the servant of all." And the mark of good servants is that they know when not to obtrude with their services. The principle of subsidiarity thus places the burden of proof on hierarchies — precisely where it should be in societies responsive to the Trinitarian vision of God.

It is tempting to dismiss the principle of subsidiarity as a political truism or perhaps another symptom of the "Constantinian hangover," a medieval conundrum as obsolete as chivalry or "noblesse oblige." Such a view, however, misses the principle's radicality, for it does not simply exhort hierarchies to serve the needs of "subordinate organizations" but insists that hierarchical structures cannot be justified apart from their "subsidiary function" in society. Here the parallels with the logic of the Trinitarian vision of God are most striking. For Catholicism recognizes a Trinity and not an infinity of Divine Persons related in the Oneness of the Divine Life, because within the community's experience of divine indwelling only two "processions" (read "subsidiary functions") can be detected. These processions, the Father's eternal "generation" of the Son, who is also the expressed Word of God, and their "spiration" or breathing forth of the Holy Spirit as the fruit of their mutual love, are constitutive of the Divine Life or, if you will, the *subsidium* of grace and peace in which, as St. Paul says, we live and move and have our being. Were more processions to be revealed, the Trinity would have to be expanded in order to accommodate the Persons active in them. The logic here is as sharp as Ockham's proverbial razor: Neither in the Divine Life nor in the organization of human society are entities to be multiplied without necessity. And note that the criteria of differentiation operative in both are analogous: there is no procession within the Divine Life unless it is manifest in the indwelling of God with us; there is no legitimate hierarchy unless it performs a "subsidiary function" among what would otherwise be an essentially egalitarian community of persons.

If the principle of subsidiarity is, along with the ideals of solidarity and participation, a reflection of the Trinitarian vision of God in Catholic social teaching, at this point, then, we may draw from an Americanist perspective two related conclusions relevant to the "New Experiment in Democracy."

First, inasmuch as the principle of subsidiarity can be derived simply from neither the aspirations of modern Western democracies nor the residual wisdom of feudalism, but is ultimately inspired by the very reality of God experienced in the divine indwelling, its applicability cannot be restricted arbitrarily to secular forms of social organization. Neither *Quadragesimo anno* nor the N.C.C.B. pastoral letters are remotely interested in exploring the meaning of subsidiarity for the church's own organization. But I contend that subsidiarity must become the basis, along with solidarity and participation, for a critique of the theory and practice of hierarchy within the Catholic church. If the principle of subsidiarity truly is a reflection of the Trinitarian vision of God, it would be ironic, to say the least, were the church to become the last place on earth in which to find it honored. Once this point is grasped, then the Americanist agenda that I'm proposing, namely, that the church's "New Experiment in Democracy" begin with the structures of the church itself, should no longer seem impertinent.

The Extraordinary Synod of Catholic bishops in Rome, held in October 1985, gives some reason to hope that this suggestion is not so odd after all. Reports from various observers, as well as the final document issued by the Synod,"The Church, in the Word of God, Celebrates the Mysteries of Christ for the Salvation of the World," indicate that not only was the principle of subsidiarity applied there to various points of ecclesiology but also its applicability was singled out for further study as part of the church's effort to understand itself as a "communion."[16] In view of the Synod, study of the "subsidiary function" may become the key to understanding such vexing problems as the operative meaning of Vatican II's call for "collegiality." The relationship, for example, between the national and regional episcopal conferences, on the one hand, and individual bishops including the Pope, on the other hand, apparently can best be understood in terms of subsidiarity. But if subsidiarity, as I have argued, means more than an exhortation to service for the hierarchy, then collegiality itself must be seen as coextensive with the whole community of faith, including ordinary lay men and women, and the hierarchy must be judged on the basis of its subsidiary function within the "college" of the People of God. Properly understood, subsidiarity will tend to encourage efforts to empower people for solidarity and participation from the bottom up, in the church just as in society as a whole.

The second conclusion is a corollary to the first. Recall Larry Rasmussen's challenge to the Catholic bishops, which saw their pastoral letter on the economy torn between two "half-formed paradigms." If the ideals of solidarity and participation and the principle of subsidiarity are understood as mirroring the Trinitarian vision of God, Rasmussen's challenge can be met without setting aside his concern that the "covenantal and eschatological nature of biblical faith . . . be carried over into the church's own self understanding." For, as we have seen, the Trinitarian paradigm knows of no fundamental incompatibility between the egalitarian and the hierarchical dimensions of human social organization. Indeed, within this paradigm the principle of subsidiarity stipulates that the differentiation of hierarchies is possible only in service to our common and fundamentally egalitarian aspirations toward self-realization. But in Rasmussen's view, the "covenantal and eschatological faith" of the Bible seems to require separating the hierarchical from the egalitarian dimensions, and repudiating the one in the name of the other. Thus, according to Rasmussen, the hierarchical tendency evident in the Israelite monarchy, though somehow still "authentically biblical," seems disposed toward idolatry and indifference to the poor, in ways that the egalitarian legacy of Exodus-Sinai astonishingly is not. Plausibly, then, the church's own historic tendency to incorporate both dimensions can be dismissed as a "Constantinian hangover." But another view, I'm arguing, is possible.

The church's tendency to keep "everyone on board dialoguing, especially the influence-wielders" is not the betrayal of "covenantal and eschatological faith," but an authentic response to the mystery of the divine indwelling within the community. But in order to grasp this point, we must clarify in what sense the Trinitarian vision of God is itself a form of "covenantal and eschatological faith." The words themselves recall our common task of building the Kingdom of God on earth: the goal is eschatological in that it transcends any form of social organization that we can devise; yet the path to it is covenantal, for the task can only be accomplished in fellowship with God. But this is precisely the point of the Trinitarian vision: the Catholic contribution to the common work of building the kingdom must stem from the church's experience of the divine indwelling. Within that experience, dialogue itself is not optional, as if it were one political stratagem among others. To keep everyone, including persons of influence, on board dialoguing, is deliberately to cultivate forms of solidarity and participation that could be just as "covenantal and eschatological" as they are truly Catholic. Admittedly, such dialogue can be corrupted into a betrayal of the inarticulate poor; but so can the repudiation of such dialogue, especially when it pretends to be the will of "the covenant-revolution-making God" disclosed in the Exodus-Sinai event.

Rasmussen is surely right to insist along with Thomas Ogletree that "an eschatological faith needs eschatological communities," and that the religious praxis of such communities should meet "a twofold requirement: 1) 'some degree of alienation from the institutional arrangements of the larger society' and 2) 'deep involvement' dedicated to 'developing qualitatively distinct alternatives to those arrangements'."[17] But I would argue that a one-sided emphasis on either the hierarchical or the egalitarian dimension is closer to the larger society's routines than any attempt to hold the two together, especially when it is governed by the principle of subsidiarity. For if subsidiarity is itself a reflection of the dynamism of the Trinitarian mystery, its ultimate meaning is eschatological; and any community that would seriously try to institutionalize this principle must become eschatological. At the very least, it will find itself involved in developing "qualitatively distinct alternatives" to the patterns of domination all too typical of the larger society.

The N.C.C.B.'s pastoral letter process, which does try to keep everyone on board dialoguing, thus strikes me as itself a religious praxis inspired by "an eschatological faith." This is especially true, I must insist, when the dialogue envisioned includes "the influence wielders" as well as the marginalized. Such dialogue, in my experience, is not typical of the larger society, and is increasingly rare even within the biblical communities of faith. The influential talk among themselves assuredly, observing carefully the protocols of well-insulated hierarchies; and the marginalized share their egalitarian dreams, if at all, only in cries and whispers that even social activists have trouble deciphering. But the silence that ensues from this interrupted conversation, though at times it may pass for civility, is fundamentally destructive of solidarity and participation. While I'm quite sure that Rasmussen does not mean to perpetuate this unhappy *status quo*, his attack upon Catholic "dialoguing," even though inspired by a genuinely biblical faith, fails to meet the eschatological criteria that he himself advocates.

For the only way to restore solidarity and to facilitate participation is to create a "qualitatively distinct alternative" in which everyone really is party to the conversation, and in which the dialogue really becomes eschatologically civil. Were I not personally convinced of its eschatological bearing, I would not be focusing so much theological attention on the pastoral letter process itself. Its procedures for adult conversation in a church that, among other things, is striving to become a community of moral discourse, though not perfect by any means, certainly are not a stratagem for coopting the marginalized and comforting the influence-wielders. Nor need they become such, if the principle of subsidiarity governs the way in which these procedures are institutionalized. Dialogue under this rubric will become a learning process in which all parties take risks in order to empower persons for the kind of solidarity and participation in which real conversation becomes possible.

Thus while I wholeheartedly support Rasmussen's call for the church "to institutionalize in its own ranks the new experiment in economic democracy," I deny that such an experiment requires any paradigm-shift away from either the pastoral letter process or the Trinitarian theology that undergirds it. On the contrary, the changes necessary for the church to make a serious commitment to the new experiment require only that the community as a whole, including its bishops, be consistent about the religious praxis implicit in the Trinitarian vision of

God. Consistency means that the "New Experiment in Democracy" will go on in the religious as well as in the political and economic spheres; it means that no issue facing the church will be taken out of the conversation and reserved for "higher authority" alone to decide. Were such an experiment actually to occur, even Rasmussen would have to certify the results as promisingly "eschatological."

In the final analysis, however, Rasmussen's misgivings cannot be set aside merely by emphasizing the eschatological promise of the pastoral letter process. His suspicions are inescapably practical, and based on the bitter wisdom that comes from a familiarity with church history: he fears that the ideals of solidarity and participation, let alone the church's professed "option for the poor," cannot be achieved within a paradigm that mystically transforms "potential theological radicals" into "prescriptive moderates." He fears, in short, that the marginalized will be sold out in a dialogue in which "influence-wielders" inevitably control the "definitions of social reality." Radical alternatives that, presumably, would be more effective in empowering the marginalized, too easily get dismissed as implausible by "responsible" decision-makers who, for the sake of the dialogue, now have a stake in keeping everyone on board. There is no theoretical perspective from which to calm these fears. As we saw in the previous chapter, the possibility of corruption, or more specifically, "systematically distorted communication," remains latent in any dialogue: it can only be laid to rest by continual scrutiny of the church's integrity as a community of moral discourse.

Understandably, similar fears have been expressed within the American Catholic community itself. Some advocates of various forms of "selective Catholicism" are even more pointed than Rasmussen in expressing skepticism about the eschatological possibilities still latent in the Trinitarian vision of God. Easily the most radical of these Catholic dissents is the one Mary Daly began in *Beyond God the Father* (1973). Her own experience of the marginality of women in a patriarchal church and a

sexist society led her to develop a way of doing theology as an act
of "liberation-castration-exorcism" for the sake of empowering
"female bonding." In ways that would occur only to a woman
steeped in traditional Catholic religious praxis, Daly has denounced the Trinitarian vision of God as "the epitome of male
bonding . . . [a] 'sublime' (and therefore disguised) erotic male
homosexual *mythos*, the perfect all-male marriage, the ideal all-
male family, the best boys' club, the model monastery, the supreme Men's Association, the mold for all varieties of male
monogender mating."[18] At stake in Daly's provocative rhetoric
is the authenticity of the Trinitarian vision: Can it actually inspire the kind of religious praxis that will empower the whole
People of God, women as well as men?

In her rage against sexist patriarchy in both the church and
society, she rejects the Trinitarian understanding of the divine
indwelling because it provides the model for "*all* patriarichal
patterning of society." The eternal processions of the Son from
the Father and the Holy Spirit from the Father and the Son, far
from liberating anyone for genuine conversation, are "the most
refined, explicit, and loaded expressions of such patterning":

> Human males are eternally putting on the masks and
> playing the roles of the Divine Persons. The mundane
> processions of sons have as their basic but unacknow-
> ledged and unattainable aim an attempted "con-
> substantiality" with the father (the cosmic father, the
> oedipal father, the professional godfather) . . . Spi-
> rated by all these relations is the asphyxiating atmo-
> sphere of male bonding. And, as Virginia Woolf saw,
> the death-oriented military processions display the
> real direction of the whole scenario, which is a funeral
> procession engulfing all life forms. God the father re-
> quires total sacrifice/destruction.[19]

Women, especially Catholic women, thus cannot empower
themselves   without   first   destroying   the   Trinitarian

paradigm,which is but a "sublime" image of "the Most Unholy Trinity: Rape, Genocide and War."

> These are structures of alienation that are self-perpetuating, eternally breeding further estrangement. The circle of destruction generated by the Most Unholy Trinity and reflected in the Unwhole Trinitarian symbol of Christianity will be broken when women, who are by patriarchal definition objects of rape, externalize and internalize a new self-definition whose compelling power is rooted in the power of being. The casting out of the demonic Trinities *is* female becoming.[20]

Given the kind of exorcism she seeks to perform, it is clear that she would reject Rasmussen's call for a return to the biblical legacy of Exodus-Sinai and, going beyond any form of "Christolatry," would invite women to create for themselves "a world without models."[21] Far more radically than Rasmussen, she is suspicious of even the possibility of inclusive "dialogue" in a sexist patriarchal society.

Daly's denunciation of the Trinity might be dismissed as mere raving, were it not true that other forms of "selective Catholicism," including perhaps the vast body of "orthodox" Catholic traditions, in fact do use this vision of God to legitimate patriarchy in both the church and society. Michael Novak's recent work, *Confessions of a Catholic*, echoes the thoughts of many neoconservatives in insisting that "the differentiation of the human sexes was used by Him — 'Father,' not 'Mother'; 'Son,' not 'Daughter' — to suggest something about His own nature."[22] Though Fatherhood and Sonship are attributed to God only analogously, for Novak the analogy remains religiously normative:

> No analogy for God's inner life is satisfactory, of course, some only less and some more so. Yet it is in-

> structive that even for eternal generation the analogy
> of Son to Father is used, and that the analogy of
> Mother to Daughter will not work. So constrained,
> the Creed chooses the one analogy, not the other.
> Whether it is a question of the incarnation of the Son
> *in history*, or of the *eternal* generation of the Son from
> the Father, in both cases the masculine imagery is
> present.[23]

Novak insists, but not very convincingly, that such imagery is
not sexist. Though the revelation of God's nature is communicated in masculine imagery, there are significant — and apparently legitimate — differences between "the ways in which
women journey toward God the Father and the ways in which
men do." Yet despite this apparent acknowledgement of a legitimate pluralism, Novak identifies a certain type of male religious
experience with the analogy canonized in the Creed:

> God the Father is a combatant. He appears to love
> with a special love those who wrestle against Him.
> Job, too, cursed Him . . . To believe in God the Father
> is not to seek peace. It is to enter into turbulent inner
> war. The peace that this God gives not only surpasses
> understanding but, altogether too often, attainment.
> To believe in Him is to accept the peace that comes
> through combat, the light that comes through harsh
> purgation.[24]

Such remarks seem to lend plausibility to Daly's identification
of the Divine indwelling with "death oriented military processions" and "the asphyxiating atmosphere of male bonding."

Novak, of course, is not simply resurrecting the Israelite
cult of Yahweh, God of battles. His *Confession of a Catholic*
means to be faithful to the Trinitarian vision of God. Yet his
theological reflections on the Trinity seem less concerned with
understanding how this doctrine emerges from Catholic reli-

gious praxis, even today, than with denouncing any apparent deviations from "orthodoxy." Thus the insights of Americanist Catholics whose own experience of the Divine Life is leading them to experiment with forms of religious praxis purged of sexism are dismissed as evidence of the new "gnosticism" that would deny the religious significance of sexual orientation. In his struggle with this all-pervasive "heresy," Novak, willy-nilly, tends to canonize the patriarchal social content latent in "orthodox" interpretations of the Trinitarian metaphors and analogies.

Novak's remarks on the Holy Spirit are especially disappointing. In an attempt to soften the impact of his uncompromising claims for the Fatherhood of God, he notes that "the symbols of the Holy Spirit often suggest the brooding, oceanic presence of the mother."[25] Yet, instead of pursuing this insight in ways that would open up the Trinitarian paradigm to the distinctive religious experiences of women, Novak recapitulates the dogmatic terminology of the Nicene Creed and commends it for its role in preserving the common biblical monotheism.[26] Furthermore, the analogies traditionally used to understand the Trinitarian processions, namely, the human person's inherent dynamism toward insight and love, are presented so abstractly that they lead less toward the divine strategy for empowering an increasingly diverse association of specific persons and communities, and more toward generalized moral exhortation:

> It [the Trinitarian vision of God] is a statement of monotheism. It is also a statement of community. It is, finally, a statement about what human beings ought to *do* in order more to live in God and more to have God live in them. They should, in short, multiply in themselves, as best they can, both in their personal lives and in their professional lives, the frequency of acts of insight, word, and love. "The kingdom of God is within you" (Luke 17:21). The more hu-

mans live the life of the spirit — the procession from
active intellect to insight, word, and love — the more
they lead God's life.[27]

The innocuous appearance of this sermonette is dispelled as
soon as it is placed in the context of Novak's remarks on the role
of male imagery in Divine revelation. In the absence of any specific tendency to the contrary, the abstract exhortations that he
builds upon the Trinitarian analogies cannot help but perpetuate the virtual monopoly on Catholic theology and religious
praxis that historically certain groups of men have enjoyed.

The problem, then, with Novak's interpretation of the
Trinitarian paradigm is as much with what he does not say, as
with what he does say. Though I cannot quarrel with his
abstractions as such, I must insist that when they are harnessed
to an attempt to discredit the Spirit's activity among the marginalized and their spokespersons, they amount to a denial of
the transformative power of the Divine Life. Novak's reflections
on the "operational meaning" of Trinitarian faith yield blandly
generalized appeals to "respect the reality of persons in community."[28] But nowhere in his *Confession of a Catholic* is there any
hint that the Trinitarian processions may be paradigmatic for
social organizations as well as for personal relationships considered in the abstract.[29] Solidarity, participation, and the principle of subsidiarity are not mentioned in this context; and
Novak's earnest desire to ferret out some hidden "gnosticism"
makes it almost impossible to discern the Spirit's presence
among those American experimenters who still hope to renew
society along these lines.

Novak's failure to see the transformative power of the
ideals and principles of Catholic social teaching is especially evident in his approach to the principle of subsidiarity. The Lay
Commission's letter, "Toward the Future," (1984) of which
Novak was the principal author, does include subsidiarity
among the chief principles of Catholic social thought; but it is

rationalized epistemologically as a necessary corollary for any decision-making process:

> This principle respects the singularity and contingency of moral decision-making and thus its prudential character. Effective decisions must accord accurately with the details and nuances of reality itself. Decisions by higher social bodies, more removed from concrete realities, almost always involve a higher degree of abstraction. Such decisions are often necessary, but they are also frequently somewhat flawed by their relative remoteness. Since Christianity is a religion firmly rooted in the mystery of the Incarnation, it must necessarily be respectful of the singular and contingent aspects of historical human reality. The principle of subsidiarity, accordingly, tries to bring decision-making as close to the texture of reality as possible.[30]

Novak and the Lay Commission are right in arguing the epistemological case for decentralized decision-making; but, again, their silence is even more telling. By not locating the principle of subsidiarity within the Trinitarian paradigm, they fail to see its potential for organizing the very structures of authority in which decisions are made. Properly understood, subsidiarity demands that hierarchical modes of organization justify their very existence; it is not just a piece of good advice suggesting how they might function more effectively.

Even more recently, Novak's *Freedom with Justice: Catholic Social Thought and Liberal Institutions* (1984) manages to discuss this tradition, including a rather detailed critique of Pope Pius XI's *Quadragesimo anno*, without so much as a mention of the principle of subsidiarity. This strange omission is understandable in light of the overall point Novak is trying to make: the critique of liberalism made by Catholic social teaching has failed because, in its zeal to refute the ideology, it has not engaged the institutions of liberal societies. When examined on their own merits, the social practices fostered by these institutions are far more consistent with the aspirations of Catholic social teaching than any that would conceivably result from the institutional arrangements occasionally proposed by the tradition itself. While Novak is justified in demanding a fair hearing for liberal institutions, the thrust of his argument forces him to ignore or to denigrate the liberal impulses already operative in Catholic social teaching.

Novak's analysis of *Quadragesimo anno* is especially crucial in this respect. This papal encyclical, written at the height of the Great Depression, is the first to confront the social conflicts characteristic of the twentieth century, the crisis in advanced industrial societies which gave rise to the ideologies of Communism, Fascism, and what Novak calls Democratic Capitalism. *Quadragesimo anno* is uncompromising in its opposition to both Soviet-style socialism and laissez-faire capitalism. The problem, then as now, is to determine whether the alternative proposed by the encyclical, usually referred to as "solidarism" or "corporatism," is anything more than an idealistic and institutionally weak form of Fascism.

Seemingly inclined to confuse it with Fascism, Novak criticizes solidarism systematically in light of both the promise and performance of liberal societies. Liberal institutions, including relatively free markets, promote democracy and social cooperation from the bottom up. Solidarism, with its state-sponsored syndicates representing various occupational groups, is pictured as intrinsically authoritarian. It tries to achieve social harmony from the top down. Novak fills out this contrast with several telling observations designed to confirm an Americanist Catholic's faith in liberal institutions.[31] But more important here is Novak's refusal to explore the specific point of Catholic resistance to Fascism, as proposed by the encyclical, namely, the principle of subsidiarity. In his eagerness to discredit solidarism, he doesn't even mention the principle, let alone explore the ways in which it might help overcome the weaknesses apparent in "solidaristic" institutions. Instead, he cites Pius XI's fears of excessive governmental intervention and notes the Pope's prayer that the system be improved though God's blessing and the more effective participation of Catholics in such institutions.

Yet, if the principle of subsidiarity had been developed as a critique of solidarism, not only would the chasm separating Catholic social teaching — even in the hands of Pius XI — from Fascist totalitarianism have been crystal clear, but also the increased public participation to which the Pope called ordinary Catholics might have been seen as a harbinger for social experiment in the direction of greater democracy. In light of the principle of subsidiarity, then, the Catholic alternative to Soviet-style communism and laissez-faire capitalism is not Fascism; but, contrary to Novak, neither is it the so-called Democratic Capitalism. It is, within whatever social system the church finds itself, to promote new experiments in participatory democracy. Admittedly, this thrust is all too obscure in *Quadragesimo anno*'s somewhat ad hoc analysis of the principle of subsidiarity; but it is fully explicit, I contend, in the N.C.C.B. pastoral letters' description of social justice in terms of "solidarity" and "participation," which expose the radical cutting edge that was always latent in the principle of subsidiarity. What this interpretation of Catholic social teaching may mean concretely when applied to both church and society in a "New American Experiment in Democracy" is the subject of the next chapter.

My differences with Michael Novak, then, are theological, though with specfic practical implications.[32] Novak and I contend, along with Mary Daly, for the meaning and continuing validity of the Trinitarian vision of God for Catholic theology and religious praxis. Daly and Novak, as I see it, represent the extremes in what is ultimately the same error regarding the Trinity. Neither begins, as Isaac Hecker does, with personal religious experience of the divine indwelling and from there learns to identify that experience with the patterns described in Trinitarian theology. Instead, both take traditional Trinitarian theology itself as the starting point, and then speculate on its possible impact on contemporary religious praxis. Because Daly sees this theology as inevitably promoting sexism, she rejects it categorically as well as the patriarchal institutions it historically has sanctioned. Because Novak means to receive this traditional theology as the *regula fidei*, or "rule of faith" predetermining Catholic religious praxis, his theological reflections seem to confer an unintended finality upon sexist patriarchy. Both extremes exhibit the same basic flaw: they lose sight of the fact that, after all, the terminology used to convey the Trinitarian vision of God is meaningless apart from the ongoing life of Catholic religious praxis.

The metaphors used to convey the experience of divine indwelling, Fatherhood, Sonship, and insight Inspirited through mutual love, are simply that: metaphors. Like any metaphors, their potential for ordering new religious experience is limited only by our willingness continually to reconsider them. But for both Daly and Novak, they seem to have become dead metaphors, but for each in a different way: They are dead for Daly because she has found it necessary to kill them in order that women may live. A new set of metaphors is needed; or, perhaps, we should try to get along with no metaphors at all. For Novak, however, they also are dying; but their death is not deliberate. Asphyxiated by the "smoke of Satan" that, alas, he conjures from the new vitality of the American Catholic church, they have become cold and stiff, blocking the flow of Divine Life rather than helping to open up new opportunities for the work of the Holy Spirit.

It remains to be seen whether even a recovery of Hecker's Americanist spirituality can preserve the Trinitarian vision of God from the death trap set for it by some of its dissenters as well as its devotees. The issues raised by Daly's repudiation of the Trinity and by Novak's defense of it are not merely of personal interest. Anyone seeking to wrestle truth from the Catholic tradition will be forced to address these issues: is the Trinitarian paradigm a dead letter, inextricably bound to the institutions of sexist patriarchy and thus justly dismissed as a theological headache accompanying the "Constantinian hangover"; or is it, as it was a century ago for Isaac Hecker, the key to fulfilling America's destiny as a truly open society? How Catholics answer these questions will, of course, determine the nature and extent of their contribution to our common task of building the Kingdom of God in America.

If the Trinitarian vision of God cannot be reconciled with the current awakening of Catholic women, then it will hardly empower the poor and uplift all the diverse peoples who make up the American republic. The Divine Life conceived through the metaphors of the Trinity, I believe, should be inclusive enough to encompass the considered aspirations of all. But the challenges posed by Daly and Novak, as well as by Rasmussen, will not be met by some theological *tour de force*. Only if Catholic religious praxis actually demonstrates the openness that, in principle, the Trinitarian vision promotes, will it once again be seen as perfecting the American destiny. The Catholic church's "New Experiment in Democracy," I have argued in this chapter, can be conducted successfully on the basis of the Trinitarian vision of God. For this perspective, better than the radically biblical alternatives proposed by Rasmussen, better than the categorical rejection of all such models advocated by Daly, and better than Novak's neo-orthodoxy, lends an ultimately theological coherence to the aspirations of Catholic social teaching, its ideals of solidarity and participation, and its principle of subsidiarity. The "New Experiment in Democracy" does not require a repudiation of these aspirations, but simply a radically consistent fulfillment of them, in the church as well as in society as a whole.

Notes

1. H. Richard Niebuhr, *The Kingdom of God in America* (New York: Harper and Row, 1959), pp. 19-20f.

2. Larry Rasmussen, "Economic Policy: Creation, Covenant and Community," in *America*, Vol. 152, No. 14 (May 4, 1985), pp. 365-7.

3. Cf. *Dogmatic Constitution on Divine Revelation (Dei Verbum)* in Walter M. Abbott, ed., *The Documents of Vatican II* (London: Geoffrey Chapman, 1967), pp. 111-128.

4. Cf. Peter Berger, *The Heretical Imperative: Contemporary Possibilities of Religious Affirmation* (Garden City, New York: Anchor Press/Doubleday, 1979), pp. 33-4.

5. Cf. "Indwelling of God," in Karl Rahner and Herbert Vorgrimler, *Theological Dictionary* (New York: Herder and Herder, 1965), pp. 227-8.

6. Cf. "Trinity," in Rahner and Vorgrimler, *op. cit.*, p. 472.

7. Cf. "Holy Ghost," in Rahner and Vorgrimler, *op. cit.*, p. 211.

8. I am using these terms in their most general anthropological sense, as described in the works of Louis Dumont, *Homo Hierarchicus: The Caste System and Its Implications* (Chicago: University of Chicago Press, 1970) and *From Mandeville to Marx: The Genesis and Triumph of Economic Ideology* (Chicago: University of Chicago Press, 1977). Dumont contrasts egalitarian and hierarchical relationships as one of the two central polarities to be accounted for in understanding society and ideology. The other polarity, which is an epistemological reflection of the first contrast, is between "holism" and "individualism." Hierarchical societies are holistic in their ideologies and individualism entails equality. I use this polarity, of course, simply in order to overcome it. My thesis is that Trinitarian theology presents a pattern that is inclusive of both hierarchical and egalitarian dimensions; and correspondingly, that Catholic social teaching typically aspires to an ideal that is inclusive of both. Furthermore, what makes the Catholic theology and social teaching interesting in the context of modern economic ideology, as Dumont describes it in *From Mandeville to Marx*, is its tendency, which I am trying to make clear and systematic, to place the burden of proof upon hierarchical forms of social organization in a society that otherwise would be consistently egalitarian. Catholicism, in short, perennially calls for a "cultural synthesis" of hierarchical and egalitarian tendencies, and thus regards any dramatic polarization of the two as problematic, though in any given situation, its concrete recommendations will emphasize one or the other of the two dimensions of the synthesis. Hence, the inevitable ambiguity of Catholic social teaching in the context of modern economic ideology.

9. Cf. "Tritheism," p. 473, and "Modalism," p. 290, in Rahner and Vorgrimler, *op. cit.*

10. National Conference of Catholic Bishops, *The Second Draft: Catholic Social Teaching and the U.S. Economy*, in *Origins*, Vol. 15, No. 17 (October 10, 1985), par. 69; *The Third Draft: Economic Justice for All: Catholic Social Teaching and the U.S. Economy*, in *Origins*, Vol. 16, No. 3 (June 5, 1986), par. 64.

11. National Conference of Catholic Bishops, *The Second Draft*, par. 82; *The Third Draft*, par. 77.

12. Pope Pius XI, *Quadragesimo anno*, par. 79, in David M. Byers, ed., *Justice in the Marketplace: Collected Statements of the Vatican and the U.S. Catholic Bishops on Economic Policy, 1891-1984* (Washington, D.C.: United States Catholic Conference, 1985), p. 68.

13. Thomas F. Duffy, *The Implications of the Papal Teaching of the Principle of Subsidiary Function for Political Theory* (Unpublished M.A. thesis, done under the supervision of Wilfrid Parsons, S.J., submitted to the Faculty of the School of Social Science, Catholic University of America, Washington, D.C., 1949), p. 25.

14. Cf. par. 119-22 in National Conference of Catholic Bishops, *The Second Draft* and *The Third Draft*.

15. National Conference of Catholic Bishops, *The Second Draft*, par. 283-313; *The Third Draft*, par. 291-321.

16. Cf. the final document of the extraordinary synod of bishops, "The Church, in the Word of God, Celebrates the Mystery of Christ for the Salvation of the World," in the *National Catholic Reporter*, (December 20, 1985), p. 16.

17. Rasmussen, *art. cit.*, p. 367.

18. Mary Daly, *Gyn/Ecology: The Metaethics of Radical Feminism* (Boston: Beacon Press, 1978), p. 38.

19. *Ibid.*, pp. 38-9.

20. Mary Daly, *Beyond God the Father: Toward a Philosophy of Women's Liberation* (Boston: Beacon Press, 1973), p. 122.

21. *Ibid.*, pp. 132-98.

22. Michael Novak, *Confession of a Catholic* (San Francisco: Harper and Row, 1983), p. 36.

23. *Ibid.*, pp. 49-50.

24. *Ibid.*, p. 36.

25. *Ibid.*, p. 38.

26. *Ibid.*, pp. 71-85.

27. *Ibid.*, p. 82.

28. *Ibid.*, p. 73.

29. Novak does discuss the Trinity in *The Spirit of Democratic Capitalism* (New York: American Enterprise Institute/Simon and Schuster, 1982), pp. 337-40, and he does try to draw an analogy between the Trinitarian pattern of "pluralism-in-unity" and the kind of "community" intended by democratic capitalism. It is strange that he did not develop this promising suggestion in his more extended treatment of the Trinity in *Confession of a Catholic*.

30. Lay Commission on Catholic Social Teaching and the U.S. Economy, *Toward the Future: A Lay Letter* (New York: American Catholic Committee, 1984), p. 6; Novak also discusses the principle of subsidiarity in *The Spirit of Democratic Capitalism*, pp. 132, 178-9, 235-6, but in none of these places does he recognize the Trinitarian foundations for this principle nor its potential for radical

social criticism. Its application seems limited to commending the virtues of small-scale entrepreneurship and greater employee involvement in corporate decision-making. When compared with the bishops' use of this principle to structure their goals for the "New American Experiment in Democracy," Novak's applications appear modest to a fault.

31. Michael Novak, *Freedom with Justice: Catholic Social Thought and Liberal Institutions* (San Francisco: Harper and Row, 1984), pp. 117, 120.

32. Novak assumes that the differences between him and his critics generally tend to be political rather than theological. I hope it is clear that the core of my criticism of Novak is theological; though, of course, it does have political implications. Cf. Novak, *Confession of a Catholic*, p. 11.

6

THE SHAPE OF THE NEW EXPERIMENT: DISCERNING THE SIGNS OF THE TIMES

The People of God believes that it is led by the Spirit of the Lord, who fills the earth. Motivated by this faith, it labors to decipher authentic signs of God's presence and purpose in the happenings, needs, and desires in which this People have a part along with other men of our age. For faith throws a new light on everything, manifests God's design for man's total vocation, and thus directs the mind to solutions which are fully human.

— *Gaudium et Spes,* Par. 11

What, then, is the shape that the "New Experiment in Democracy" ought to take in view of this Americanist interpretation of the Trinitarian vision of God? This question cannot be answered simply by recalling what the Americanist agenda was, either at the founding of the Republic or at the point of its condemnation by Rome. For the nation clearly is not the same as it was then, and neither are the aspirations of the American Catholic community. But just as clearly it cannot be answered simply by taking the current pulse of the nation and the Catholic community within it. For the Americanist agenda is not, and never was, merely a baptism of the *Zeitgeist.* Now, as then, it must emerge through what Vatican II described as a reading of "the signs of the times." In order, therefore, to detect some initial

157

sense of practical direction for the "New American Experiment," it is necessary to examine Vatican II's formulation more carefully and ask just who in the church has a right to interpret the signs of the times.

What Vatican II had to say about this new form of theological interpretation is tantalizing, but not fully illuminating. Responding to cues given by Pope John XXIII as he called the Council together, *Gaudium et Spes* speaks of the church's "duty of scrutinizing the signs of the times and of interpreting them in the light of the gospel."[1] The term, "signs of the times," echoes words attributed to Jesus in the Synoptic Gospels,[2] which seem to refer to concrete indications of the Messianic era that most of Jesus' audience somehow had missed. In the Council's usage both the note of accusation and the Messianic expectation are muted. Scrutinizing the signs of the times becomes a perennial "duty" of the whole People of God: in order to "carry forward the work of Christ Himself under the lead of the befriending Spirit," the church must "recognize and understand the world in which we live, its expectations, its longings, and its often dramatic characteristics."[3] By shifting the focus of concern from the Messiah to the world in which his work must be accomplished, Vatican II thus clearly committed the Catholic church to the project that H. Richard Niebuhr described as building the "kingdom on earth."

Though the Council's *Gaudium et Spes* was abstractly theoretical in identifying these signs, it did provide an example of how such a scrutiny of the world should proceed. This "Pastoral Constitution on the Church in the Modern World," following up on the generous appeals of Pope John, began its discussion of Catholic social teaching with a fundamentally optimistic assessment of the technological, social, and psychological changes characteristic of modernity. While also recognizing certain "imbalances in the modern world," *Gaudium et Spes* emphasized the positive impact of these changes upon the "broader desires" of the whole human race. In particular, it stressed that "now, for the first time in human history, all people are convinced that the benefits of culture ought to be and actually can be extended to everyone."[4] This "thirst for a full and free life worthy of man" within a world that reverences the global interdependence of persons and nations, in other circles may be discounted as another "revolution of rising expectations." But instead of throwing a dash of cold water on this revolution, the Council affirms it as "the marvelous providence" of God working to renew the face of the earth.[5] The "signs of the times" thus are seen as raising the questions, both practical and theoretical, to which the church must respond as if to God's own presence in the world. Discerning their meaning proceeds on the same assumption as that of the Americanists who perceived the work of the Holy Spirit, not just in the church but also in society as a whole.

With all the excitement generated during and after Vatican II by this fresh approach to religious discernment in Catholic practical theology, it apparently did not occur to the Council fathers to define more precisely who does the discerning, and in cases of conflict, whose reading of "the signs of the times" is to prevail. Pope John XXIII had exercised his papal prerogatives in this area by convoking the Council as he did; but just as clearly *Gaudium et Spes*, following the lead of the bishops who intervened to make the Council their own, affirms that the church as a whole has the duty of interpreting these "signs."[6] One possible resolution of the not-so-hypothetical conflict over authority implicit in these separate initiatives has been offered by Pope John Paul II. Repeatedly he has insisted that adherence to the papal *magisterium* is "an indispensable condition for the proper interpretation of the 'signs of the times'." But Peter Hebblethwaite has convincingly argued that such an outcome, in effect, is less an interpretation of the Conciliar teaching than its annulment.

> To reduce it [the church's duty of reading the signs of the times] to a function of the central authority is to bowdlerize the text and domesticate the doctrine. It

makes the local churches once more dependent on the
center, it deprives them of initiative, and it suggests
that the study of local situations can be replaced by
judgments emanating effortlessly from the *magisterium*. This is the most "reactionary" statement ut-
tered by John Paul. But since everyone knows it is
unworkable, perhaps it does not matter.[7]

But it does matter; for unless the whole People of God, and not
just the Pope, is involved in formulating the church's agenda in
the world, then our hopes for the church becoming a genuine
community of moral discourse are in vain, and the pastoral letters' preaching of social justice as participation will sound, to
paraphrase St. Paul, like a gong booming or a cymbal clashing.
The church's continuing inability to be consistent about who has
the right to interpret "the signs of the times" may be the single
biggest obstacle confronting the "New American Experiment in
Democracy."

From an Americanist perspective, consistency obviously requires that the local churches, rather than the Vatican bureaucracy, must bear primary responsibility for interpreting the
signs of the times. For if the signs themselves are generally
local, so must the church's responses to them be. When, not if,
conflicts of interpretation arise within the local churches, they
are to be resolved through processes of spiritual discernment,
however protracted and difficult, at the local level. Correspondingly, when conflicts arise among the various local churches,
they are to be resolved not through unilateral intervention on
the part of the Vatican, but through the regular Synods of
bishops in communion with Rome or, if need be, through additional ecumenical Councils. The Americanist agenda thus rests,
as it always has, on the premise that a "certain liberty" not only
can be permitted in church, but is also positively to be encouraged. If the principle of subsidiarity means anything at all, it
means freedom within the church for the local churches to discern their own agendas in the world, a freedom to make their

own distinctive contributions to the building of the Kingdom of God.

That this expectation of a "certain liberty" in reading the signs of the times is not simply an anomaly attributable to American Catholicism's overwhelmingly "middle class" character should be evident from the experiences of other local churches, particularly those of the Netherlands and of Latin America. Though progressive Dutch Catholicism now survives more or less in a state of siege, the Brazilian bishops' conference, along with other Latin American bishops, notably in Peru, so far have successfully resisted pressures from the Vatican to condemn out-of-hand indigenous movements, like liberation theology, and theologians, like Gustavo Gutierrez and Leonardo Boff, who speak for them. The refusal of these bishops to knuckle under, so reminiscent of the skillful maneuvers of Cardinal Gibbons in trying to protect Edward McGlynn — and so very unlike the actions of the current Board of Trustees at Catholic University in Washington, D.C., toward Charles E. Curran — this episcopal dissent amounts to a reassertion of the local churches' right to act responsibly in scrutinizing "the signs of the times."

The responsible exercise of that "certain liberty" may be countered, as it was in the Netherlands, by vigorous exploitation of the Vatican's effective control of episcopal appointments. If the recent events in the Seattle archdiocese are any indication,[8] inquisitions thinly veiled as "collegial" visitations will occur, followed by the consecration of "auxiliary" bishops who can be counted on in Rome to impose the current mood emanating from the papal *magisterium*. But this tactic, as egregious as it is a cynical attack upon the Council's spirit of collegiality, must be resisted collectively by the national episcopal conferences. For the Vatican's effective control over episcopal appointments, to whatever ends it may be applied, arguably, is a violation of the principle of subsidiarity.

This struggle over the right to interpret "the signs of the times" within the Catholic church worldwide is itself one of the signs of the times. It suggests that the Holy Spirit is active in the local churches throughout the world, and not just in the palaces of the Vatican. It makes clear that the rising expectations of humanity which Vatican II found so providential cannot be kept outside the church. For the local church in the United States it means that the bishops' call for a "New American Experiment in Democracy" cannot be implemented in society unless that "certain liberty" in setting the church's agenda is exercised by the whole People of God. The democratization of the church, therefore, is the only guarantee that the church will be free to interpret the signs of the times.

Given how virtually every theological theme we have considered so far, solidarity and participation, the principle of subsidiarity, and the duty of scrutinizing the signs of the times, seems to converge toward a new experiment in democracy first of all *within* the church, it is important to understand that this experiment is truly rooted in the traditions of Americanist Catholicism. As we recall from chapter one, the Americanist "heresy" as such was not about democracy within the church, but its condemnation surely stemmed in part from Rome's fear of any experimentation with democracy. One needs, therefore, to dig deeper into American Catholic history in order to recover the context in which democratization itself becomes an issue. Historian Jay Dolan's recent description of the "republican blueprint" for the church originally envisioned by John Carroll, the first Catholic bishop consecrated for service in revolutionary America, provides us with an appropriately dangerous memory of our democratic aspirations.

Consistent with what later became known as the principle of subsidiarity, Carroll originally asserted that the only way the American Catholic church could maintain its integrity against foreign interference would be for the local clergy, representing the whole People of God, to elect its bishops. The early struggles within the emerging national church over this policy, when coupled with the various conflicts at the parish level over lay "trusteeism," must be seen as an authentically Catholic experiment in democracy, however premature. Historians point out in hindsight, of course, that the experiment was virtually doomed to fail from the start, and not just because of the machinations of the Vatican bureaucracy.[9] But the "republican blueprint" operative in it remained there for future generations of Americanist Catholics to make their own, and the signs of the times, as I read them, suggest that now is the time to try again.

I wish to emphasize the fundamentally Catholic thinking behind what Dolan calls the "republican blueprint" for the church. For unless its Catholic roots are appreciated, this attempt to begin the "New American Experiment in Democracy" by transforming the structures of the church could plausibly be dismissed as another "foreign" imposition. The argument for "trusteeism" or lay participation in the governance of the local churches is especially significant here. In 1818, Dr. Matthew O'Driscoll and the trustees of the parish at Charleston, South Carolina, for example, presented a defense of their position based on the *jus patronatus* traditionally enjoyed by the Catholic sovereigns of Europe.[10] These princes had exercised this "right of patronage" by supervising the governance of the church in their territory through the nomination of bishops and other ecclesiastical office holders. O'Driscoll argued that since this right was exercised on the basis of legitimate sovereignty, it should not be forfeited simply because in the United States such sovereignty rested ultimately with "We the People" and not with a territorial prince.

Indeed, inasmuch as the revolutionary Constitution of the United States provided for the separation of church and state, the *ius patronatus* in principle could *not* be exercised by the government but had to fall to that portion of the American people who actually form the Catholic community here:

> [That] part of the sovereign people of these United States, in communion with His Holiness, the Pope . . . think, and hold themselves, *immediately* entitled, to the same benefits and immunities in their

religious concerns as are established between the
court of Rome and the Sovereigns of Europe, *im-
mediately* negotiating for the interests and religious
liberties of their subjects.[11]

O'Driscoll seems to be saying that, if the Vatican has traditionally conceded a *ius patronatus* to Catholic princes, it cannot,
without contradicting itself, fail to recognize that this right ultimately belongs to the Catholic community as a whole. Democratization, in other words, at least in the sense of lay participation in the election of bishops and pastors, thus is rooted in
Catholic tradition. But with the paradigm shift to popular
sovereignty initiated by the American revolution, the time had
become ripe to expand lay participation from the Catholic
sovereigns of Europe to the whole People of God.

O'Driscoll's brilliant insight into the full implications of the
American revolution for the ecclesiastical polity of the Catholic
church, of course, was unacceptable to the Vatican. In the wake
of the French revolution, the Napoleonic wars, and the restoration of the papacy in Rome, the moderate "Gallicanism" which
evidently shaped O'Driscoll's assumptions about the role of the
laity in the church was rapidly giving way to the reactionary,
but nevertheless innovative, ideology of "Ultramontanism."
Rather than extend to the whole People of God the *ius patronatus* that Gallicanism had championed for the French aristoc-
racy, the Vatican and its Ultramontanist admirers hoped to
save postrevolutionary Europe by grounding all authority,
political as well as spiritual, in the papacy. This unprecedented
and all-too-typically modern centralization of authority envisioned by Ultramontanism was to culminate in the definition
of Papal Infallibility accepted at Vatican I (1869-70). The historic movement toward this centerpiece in the ideology of papal
domination was already underway before O'Driscoll and his associates had a chance to make their case.

Catholics acting from an Americanist perspective, however,
have good reasons not to regard O'Driscoll's lay "trusteeism" as

a lost cause. While most of us were just awakening to the death of the immigrant church, far-sighted reformers had already understood that the logic of Vatican II, if allowed to reach a successful conclusion, could only result in the democratization of the post-Conciliar church. Americanist Catholics should well understand that when Hans Küng emphasized the need for "truthfulness" within the church, he concluded in behalf of all of us that democratization would be necessary.[12] For just as clearly as the young John Carroll and the lay trustees, Küng saw that a Catholic church truly responsive to presence of the Holy Spirit in its own local communities must provide for the free election of its leaders. But unlike Carroll who, for a number of historically defensible reasons, envisioned this electoral process as the exclusive prerogative of the clergy,[13] Küng insists that in our own time the right of free election must be exercised by the whole People of God, including the laity.

Very clearly responsive to the delicate balance of egalitarian and hierarchical tendencies called for in the principle of subsidiarity, Küng's proposal, like the "republican blueprint" of Carroll and the lay trustees, maintains a distinctively Catholic loyalty to the papacy. One Americanist expression of this loyalty, while calling for the establishment of a "National American Church, with liberties consonant to the spirit of the Government, under which [we] live," also insists on "due obedience in essentials to the Pontifical Hierarchy."[14] The young Carroll knew such loyalty was due the pope "as Spiritual head of the Church." But more to the point, he argued that the recognition of the pope's spiritual leadership constituted "the only connexion [American Catholics] ought to have with Rome."[15] In advocating the democratization of the church, Küng himself asserts that "the final authority of the parish priest, bishop and pope should be expressly maintained in order to avoid a general paralysis of the different forces."[16] Though the "essentials" recognized by Carroll and the lay trustees and the "final authority" conceded by Küng are not entirely clear, the loyalty of the intention standing behind them should be: the "republican blueprint" is not meant to force the Catholic church into schism, but to exercise "that Ecclesiastical liberty, which," in Carroll's words, "the temper of the age and of our people requires."[17]

The details of Küng's proposal are worth reviewing here, for, in light of the American Catholic church's recent experience in organizing massive consultations like "Call to Action" and the bishops' pastoral letter process, what he envisions is certainly not beyond the organizational capabilities of the church today. Democratization would consist primarily in building mechanisms of downward accountability into the structures of the church to balance the Vatican's mechanisms of upward accountability. Küng specifically recommends an interlocking structure of representative bodies, ranging from worldwide councils of bishops and laity to the various committees of the local parish councils, each invested with the right of free election of its own religious leadership.[18] The Pope would be elected by the worldwide councils of bishops and laity, which in turn are elected by the various diocesan pastoral councils, which also in turn are elected by the clergy and the laity of the local parish churches. Consistent with the principle of subsidiarity, the electoral process thus would work from bottom up; but it would also form a hierarchy constituted for service who, once installed in office for a specified term, would have the executive authority necessary to work with the decisions of the groups they have been chosen to lead. It is hard to imagine how the task of setting the church's agenda in the world can actually be shared among the whole People of God, apart from some such proposal for the popular election of its religious leadership.

The Americanist agenda, however, is not exhausted by arguing the case for the democratization of the church on the basis of the "republican blueprint" that inspired the distinct but related strategies of the young John Carroll and the lay trustees. Though such a retrieval is the indispensable precondition for carrying out Vatican II's program of scrutinizing "the signs of the times," an authentically Americanist Catholic church must point beyond itself to the public consequences of its "New Amer-

ican Experiment in Democracy." To understand these consequences we must turn from the narrower concerns of Catholic
ecclesiology and church history and ask what is the significance
of this experiment for our common task of building the Kingdom
of God in America.

Many informed observers, including more recently Protestant theologians and social critics Martin Marty, Parker
Palmer, Richard John Neuhaus, and Robert Bellah,[19] have argued on various premises that the original American experiment in democracy may be in serious trouble these days. Though
they disagree among themselves on specific points of analysis
and on proposed solutions, they all seem to be pointing to a crisis
in the public order involving our very capacities to think and act
as citizens of a democracy. They are also one in thinking that
this crisis has been exacerbated by the decline of the mainline
American religious communities since the 1960s, and that any
solution to the crisis will involve the renewal of these communities in some form of "public church." Their own keen interest in the Catholic church's "New American Experiment in
Democracy" stems from this sense of impending crisis.

At the core of their diagnoses stands an ongoing dialogue
with Alexis de Tocqueville, the French Catholic aristocrat
whose report on his travels here in the 1830s, *Democracy in
America*, remains an indispensable point of departure for any
reading of "the signs of times" in this country. As one whose own
family had fallen victim to the excesses of the French revolution,
Tocqueville sought to understand why democracy in America,
based upon theories of popular sovereignty not unlike those appealed to in France, had not produced similarly dubious results.
His analysis provides two themes of central importance to current discussion of religion and democracy in America. First, he
emphasized the role played by the distinctively American form
of Christianity in sustaining a passion for democracy, but not
revolution, in the United States. Second, he speculated on the
possibilities for an unprecedented kind of despotism lurking in
this new egalitarian form of government:

I seek to trace the novel features under which despotism may appear in the world. The first thing that
strikes the observation is an innumerable multitude
of men, all equal and alike, incessantly endeavoring
to procure the petty and paltry pleasures with which
they glut their lives. Each of them, living apart, is as
a stranger to the fate of all the rest; his children and
his private friends constitute to him the whole of
mankind . . . . Above this race of men stands an im-
mense and tutelary power, which takes upon itself
alone to secure their gratifications and to watch over
their fate. That power is absolute, minute, regular,
provident, and mild. It would be like the authority of
a parent if, like that authority, its object was to prepare men for manhood; but it seeks, on the contrary,
to keep them in perpetual childhood: it is well content
that the people should rejoice, provided they think of
nothing but rejoicing . . . . Thus it every day renders
the exercise of the free agency of man less useful and
less frequent; it circumscribes the will within a narrower range and gradually robs a man of all the uses
of himself.[20]

The current discussion goes beyond Tocqueville in linking
this prophecy of "administrative despotism" with the systemic
crisis of the modern Welfare State. Virtually all these critics,
whatever their current political orientations, recognize the
problems of the welfare state in Tocqueville's cryptic fear of
what might result from the mass pursuit of narrow self-interest
in an indiscriminately egalitarian society. The apparent decline
of popular participation in politics and in the various activities
that sustain the civic community, and the marked deterioration
in the quality of public argument over the past generation in
this country, when correlated with the rise of "Big Government,"
its unsustainable levels of public expenditure, its inefficiencies,
and, above all, its negative impact upon the capacities of all citi-

zens to govern themselves responsibly, all are seen as fulfilling Tocqueville's bleak prophecy.

When correlated with the decline in participation in the churches of so-called "mainline" Protestantism, a trend sometimes noted since the mid-1960s in Catholicism as well, these symptoms of crisis seem to confirm Tocqueville's insight into the way in which American religious communities help sustain a democratic ethos. The ever-present possibility of "administrative despotism" waxes and wanes in proportion to the vitality of American religious communities engaged in the common task of building "the kingdom on earth." In those periods of our history when the "mainline" religious communities are strong, democratic institutions generally are strong; but also correspondingly weak when these communities are in disarray. Understanding Tocqueville's insight, of course, is crucial, if the church's "New Experiment in Democracy" is to be of more than parochial interest.

Within this shared Tocquevillean consensus, however, these Protestant commentators disagree as to what precisely has caused the recent decline in the "mainline" religious communities, and how the renewal of American Christianity once more might be promoted in order to minimize the threat of "administrative despotism." These disagreements naturally tend to reflect the ideological struggle currently working itself out in the mainstream of American politics, namely, the rise of neoconservatism as an alternative to the liberal progressivism that had been dominant since the time of Roosevelt's New Deal. As Peter Steinfels has convincingly argued,[21] at the core of what is distinctively neoconservative is a thesis about a "New Class" that, within the framework of the New Deal welfare state, now embodies the contagion of "administrative despotism."

This "New Class," constituted for the most part by those 1960s student activists who have slowly wormed their way into positions of public responsibility, stands accused of promoting the kind of egalitarian "cultural chaos" that can only perpetuate a need for the services of an expanding welfare state. By failing to reinforce the efforts of local communities to restore "social discipline," the "New Class," for all its idealism, actually undermines the capacities of ordinary citizens to govern themselves. Like any other form of parasitic infection, the "New Class," according to neoconservatives, makes its living off the "chaos" that its own ostensibly reformist activities inevitably generate.[22] Any solution to the crisis in American democracy therefore must begin by eliminating or at least significantly reducing the influence of the "New Class" over this nation's public life.

The disagreement between liberal progressives and neoconservatives within America's "mainline" religious communities, however, seems to boil down to whether this "New Class" or the equally problematic religious "New Right" is the greater threat to the renewal of American Christianity. Though neoconservative religious intellectuals, like Peter Berger, Richard John Neuhaus, and Michael Novak, are quick to dramatize any evidence of the "New Class" phenomenon within the churches, other religious observers, like those who support Norman Lear's "People for the American Way," see the rise of a religious "New Right" as more threatening. What makes the "New Right" new is that it represents that part of the Protestant evangelical community that heretofore has not been very active in the nation's public life. Religious liberals fear the "New Right" not so much because they disagree with their positions on specific policy questions, but because they are not sure whether they share with them any tacit agreements about the nature of either the Kingdom of God or the American experiment in democracy, within which to argue their disagreements.

The fears of religious liberals thus focus on the principle of separation of church and state, and the pluralistic society that it necessarily entails. Does the religious "New Right" respect this principle as itself part of the work of building "the kingdom on earth," or would it use the state as an instrument to enforce a "social discipline" on all communities consistent with its own sectarian vision of a "Christian America"? This is the question, of course, that stands behind liberal resistance to "New Right" social issues, such as its lobbying for a "Right to Life" amendment to the U.S. Constitution. The point of this resistance, especially on the part of those who personally disapprove of abortion, is not just to repudiate single-issue politics.

Socially activist religious groups in America, seeking from all points on the political spectrum to build "the kingdom on earth," have always tended to organize their supporters on a single issue. This is especially true of the progressive movements with which religious liberals identify: the abolitionists, the suffragettes, those who favored prohibition, the civil rights movement, the protesters against American involvement in the Vietnamese civil war, and, most recently, the nuclear freeze movement. It would thus be sheer hypocrisy for religious liberals to denounce the "New Right" for single-issue politics. Religious liberals, who appreciate this point, base their resistance instead on the failure of the "New Right" to demonstrate its commitment to the principle of separation of church and state, and the limits which that principle imposes on the government's own powers of social intervention. For all its trumpeted opposition to "Big Government," would the "New Right" use the apparatus of the welfare state to enforce a Christian "administrative despotism" of its own?

Neoconservatives, on the other hand, seem unimpressed by the fears of religious liberals. In their view, religious liberals have become collaborators with the "New Class" who, in addition to their other crimes, allegedly would use the principle of separation of church and state to undermine, if not eliminate, the influence of any religious community upon the nation's public life. Thus despite, or perhaps precisely because of, the failure of religious liberals, neoconservatives are making overtures to the religious "New Right" in order to conduct a guerrilla campaign against the "New Class" ideology of "secular humanism" and its alleged hegemony in the nation's public life. If liberal religious activists cannot see their way into such a coalition, then so much the worse for liberal religious activists. Let them be marginalized.

Nowhere is this neoconservative strategy more evident than in Richard John Neuhaus' recent book, *The Naked Public Square: Religion and Democracy in America*. Like most promising ideologies in our society, Neuhaus' construction trades upon ambiguity. He is critical of "politicized fundamentalism," but he also denigrates "pluralism" as a "jealous god." While Neuhaus thus tries to position himself as a critic of the whole spectrum of religiously oriented ideologies, his argument does seem to be moving in a coherently neoconservative direction: The public square, that is, our collective capacities for democratic self-government, recently has been stripped naked, because of the failure of American religious communities, especially those of the "mainstream," to act responsibly in public life. In their unthinking passion for the "liberal" cause of the moment, these communities have obscured, if not actually betrayed, liberalism's underlying commitment to truly democratic processes in politics and government. In other words, they have helped erode the cultural foundations of democracy, for democracy in America cannot be sustained on a naked public square. Clothing the naked public square, for Neuhaus, ultimately involves forging a coalition which must include elements of the religious "New Right."

What Neuhaus presents in the book, however, is not so much a blueprint for the new coalition as an ideological rationale for one. Like other modern ideologies, at its core Neuhaus' contains a myth about history, in this case the restoration of a "Christian America." To sustain this myth he must, of course, discount systematically the impact of the Enlightenment upon this nation's "Founding Fathers" and the federalist structures that they managed to create. This he does whenever he gets the opportunity, but his point in doing so is not historical; it is simply to instill in his readers the notion, repeated several times throughout the book, that America is not now, nor has it ever been, a "secular society": "Loyalty to the *civitas* can safely

be nurtured only if the *civitas* is not the object of highest loyalty."[23] To think otherwise in the American context is to "deny
who we are."[24] It is also to deny, by implication, the Tocquevillean premise about the relationship between religion and democracy that Neuhaus shares with religious liberals.

The ponderous assertion of such denials, however, turns
out to be more provocative than it is illuminating. Though
Neuhaus seems willing to defend both the ideal of a "Christian
America" and the reality of religious and cultural pluralism, he
is not yet as clear as, say, H. Richard Niebuhr on how to bring
the two together for the sake of some new cultural synthesis.[25]
Neither the secularity of our public institutions, nor the ideology of American "civil religion," nor even the virtue of civility
come off well here. While the religious "New Right" is advised to
become more politically responsible, even to the point of adapt-
ing the mainstream's political ethic of "compromise,"[26] Neuhaus
also denounces a "pragmatism" identified with "interest-group
liberalism" as "fatal to the church's witness."[27] Clarity usually
comes when Neuhaus is disparaging his "New Class" enemies:
secular humanists and their allies within mainline liberal Protestantism, especially as these have insitutionalized themselves within the National Council of Churches.

Interestingly enough in this context, Neuhaus displays a
special solicitude for American Catholics. He quotes selectively,
but admiringly, from John Courtney Murray on American religious and cultural pluralism, but insists that Murray's insight
into the religious foundations of the American experiment in democracy is more likely to find an echo today, despite his expressed confidence in liberal Protestantism, among the religious
"New Right."[28] This rather strained conjecture is typical of
Neuhaus' overall approach to Catholicism. Ever zealous to en-
list Catholics in his campaign to clothe the naked public square,
Neuhaus would urge Catholics simultaneously to remain innocent of the "visceral reaction to Protestant fundamentalism"
that keeps mainline Protestantism from renewing its traditional commitment to the ideal of a "Christian America," and to

be wary of any innovations like the pastoral letter process that in Neuhaus' view tend to encourage Catholics to work more closely with liberal Protestants.[29] Given Neuhaus' view of the public square, these exhortations make sense as part of a bid to broker some new ecumenical coalition: If the "New Class" is to be defeated, liberal Protestants must be isolated, while Catholics, Lutherans, and the more politically and theologically sophisticated elements of the religious "New Right," including Rev. Jerry Falwell's "Moral Majority," must unite in a common front to restore to the public square the sacred canopy of a "Christian America."

My disagreements with Neuhaus are as narrow as our agreements are broad. Though his recognition that ours may be a special "'Catholic moment' in American religious and cultural history" is similar to the one animating this book, we disagree over how the church might best prepare itself to act responsibly in this moment. What I find most promising in the church, namely, the bishops' pastoral letter process and its potential for creating among Catholics a genuine community of moral discourse, he fears because it may follow "the Protestant mainline churches along the path toward cultural and political marginality."[30] The pastoral letters' new kind of collegial leadership that I hope will develop into a consistent agenda for the democratization of the church, Neuhaus, along with the Catholic neoconservatives, seems to regard as a troubling symptom of the "clericalization of political discourse." While I cannot help but sympathize with his call to all Americans to exercise a "critical patriotism," I must insist that such is precisely the point of this Americanist Catholic effort to participate in the common task of building "the kingdom on earth." If Neuhaus is serious about the "Catholic moment" in American history, he ought to stop supporting attempts to undermine the pastoral letter process either through guilt by association with liberal Protestantism, or through blanket charges misappropriating our common fears about the politicization of religion.

Even assuming that the cluster of problems that Neuhaus has identified as a naked public square are real, I fail to see how the kind of coalition building that he urges is likely to resolve them. What sense does it make to isolate liberal Protestantism, when this group of mainstream churches represents the one uninterrupted Christian source of critical patriotism since the founding of the republic? Hasn't Neuhaus' fear of the "New Class" clouded his judgment regarding the "New Right's" ambivalence toward religious pluralism? Doesn't the myth of a "Christian America" encourage that ambivalence just as much as the equally misleading myths of secular humanism against which the religious "New Right" is in revolt? Beyond all these misgivings, however, stands what I take to be the basic dilemma confronting Neuhaus: if the nation's public life has really become as decadent as he contends it has, no religious coalition, however shrewdly put together, would ever be sufficient to restore its integrity. For if the public square no longer embodies a deep consensus about the meaning of the American experiment in democracy, then all such coalition-building is, at the very least, premature. Though Neuhaus may be commended for helping to open up dialogue between some of the "mainstream" churches and the religious "New Right," the crisis that he had hoped to resolve can only be addressed by working to restore that deep consensus.

Rather than aim directly at renewing a "Christian America," American religious communities, Catholic as well as Protestant, are more likely to rediscover the basis for that consensus by renewing themselves as a "public church." This term, coined by Martin Marty, refers to an agenda at once more modest and more promising than Neuhaus': it proposes that America's Christian churches rediscover themselves as a "communion of communions" operating within the framework of this nation's political "community of communities."[31] While pointedly agnostic on the subject of a "Christian America," such a communion remains "especially sensitive to the *res publica*, the public order that surrounds and includes people of faith."[32]

Though it may become institutionalized as a coalition including the liberal Protestant mainline, Catholicism, and what Marty inclusively describes as "the newer evangelicalism," the "public church" is less a strategy for coalition-building and more a collective learning process for cultivating the churches' common "faith in civility."[33]

Besides being politically necessary, "civility" thus turns out to be a religious virtue. Its faithful exercise makes each of the communions participating in the American "public church," as well as their respective members, more disposed to regard each other in public as mutually interdependent, as bound to each other, in Marty's terms, *"by explicit or tacit agreement, to mutual communication, of whatever is useful and necessary for the harmonious exercise of social life'* . . . . "[34] "Civility" thus is the ecumenical virtue *par excellence*; for in our pluralistic context, it is the indispensable precondition for building the Kingdom of God in America. Pluralism may exist without "civility," but a pluralistic society cannot, if it lacks the sense of social interdependence which this virtue fosters among diverse communities who, both because of and in spite of their differences, remain pledged to one another for the sake of the common good.

The "public church," then, is merely the process that institutionalizes the practice of civility within the Christian "communion of communions" in order to promote "the harmonious exercise of [this nation's] social life." Like Neuhaus' coalition for a "Christian America," the "public church" also embodies the common Tocquevillean premise. But it seeks to avoid "administrative despotism," not by mobilizing a political struggle both inside and outside the churches against the real or imagined threat of a "New Class," but by promoting the renewal in each church of those institutional practices and learning processes that actually empower Christians for more effective participation in the common task of building the "kingdom on earth." Such a strategy, at once more radical and yet more ideologically agnostic than Neuhaus', also seems to be more faithful to Tocqueville's pioneering insights into the relationship between religion and democracy in America.

Participation in the "public church" thus is not reserved for card-carrying members of either the "New Class" or the religious "New Right." Nor is one required to confess liberal Protestantism in order to join; but, then, neither is one required to recant it. All that is required is a heightened sense of our mutual interdependence, especially in matters spiritual and ecclesial, sufficient to make a "communion of communions" seem both necessary and possible. Even so, to join the "public church" is not to change denominations, but to encourage institutional development within one's own denomination as part of this "symbiotic" process. Catholics and evangelicals who awaken to the reality of the "public church" do not thereby lose their distinctive identities; but they do embark upon a process of discernment that may lead them to discover their own communion's unique contribution to the American experiment in democracy.

Within the Catholic communion in this country, the Americanist agenda continues to provide the litmus test of Catholicism's response to the call of the "public church." As I have outlined it earlier, the history of Americanist Catholicism has shown as much ambivalence about the ideal of a "Christian America" as the "mainstream" Protestant denominations have. Isaac Hecker's dream of converting the American nation as a whole to Catholicism, no doubt, was inspired by the same missionary zeal that once animated Protestant dreams of a "Righteous Empire." Yet, like the Protestant mainline, Americanist Catholics also came to embrace the Providential meaning of the principle of separation of church and state, and the limits it must place on any enthusiasm for a "Christian America." Even so, if the Tocquevillean fear of "administrative despotism" is at all justified, the challenge confronting the "public church" today is not whether the public life of this nation shall be patterned according to the ideals of a "Christian America," but whether together we can nurture and preserve for America any public life at all. What can Americanist Catholics contribute to the "public church's" effort to meet this challenge?

The answer lies in their possible contribution to the collective learning process. As I have been arguing throughout this book, the Americanist agenda lives again today on the promise of the U.S. Catholic bishops' recent pastoral letters. Far more important than any of the letters' substantive recommendations in the area of Christian morality and public policy is the adult moral dialogue that the bishops have stimulated in preparing the letters. While the bishops may have seen the public dialogue initially only as useful for establishing their own competence in matters of public policy, through it they have grown unexpectedly into a style of episcopal moral leadership appropriate to a pluralistic democracy. Though the debates over the pastoral letters have been vigorous and absorbing, involving both laity and clergy, Catholic and nonCatholic alike, from an Americanist perspective what is most promising about them is that partisans on all sides of the issues have become more skillful in public argument, more acutely aware of the complexities of public policy questions, yet also less reluctant to contribute to the task of finding answers to them. In short, those who have participated in the pastoral letter process have empowered themselves for democratic self-government.

More effectively than any Catholic social teaching on this subject, the pastoral letter process itself has fostered certain virtues indispensable to citizenship in a pluralistic democracy, not the least of which is civility in the service of social responsibility. In the face of the threat of an "administrative despotism" masquerading as government by technical expertise, the pastoral letters have liberated national defense and economic questions for genuinely *public* policy discussion. The enervating myth that declares such questions too complex for ordinary citizens to understand was dispelled, and so was the virtual monopoly on policy-making exercised by the new priesthood of government bureaucrats. Nowhere has the struggle against such myth been more dramatic than in the bishops' discussion of nuclear deterrence and related issues. Where taboos about atomic secrets had once effectively removed these issues from civil discourse, informed debate among ordinary citizens now became commonplace.

What the bishops contributed to the various movements which have reawakened a sense of critical patriotism among the citizenry is a self-correcting process of mutual learning and teaching, which promises not only to strengthen our capacities for democratic consensus-making, but also to insure that whatever consensus we achieve will be informed by religious and ethical considerations. In an Americanist perspective, this learning process, if consistently implemented, could transform the Catholic church into a community of moral discourse. While Americanist Catholics know only too well how revolutionary this transformation may have to be, fortified by a sense of participation in the work of the "public church," they also see themselves as sharing a gift already given. For the pastoral letter process is only a Catholic response internalizing the sense of interdependence and the procedures of mutual accountability, especially in matters affecting the common good, that have always been characteristic of the ideals, at least, of the American "public church." There may be Providential irony, however, in the fact that this new Catholic contribution comes at a time when the Protestant mainline is most in need of renewing its commitment to the "public church."

It would be foolish to claim that the Americanist Catholic church alone is now poised to save this nation from the threat of "administrative despotism." Social movements especially responsive to this threat, from a variety of religious and secular perspectives, have been promoting any number of American experiments in participatory democracy. The pastoral letter process is uniquely promising because the Catholic community is becoming an increasingly visible part of the mainstream of American public life. If that community should succeed with its "New Experiment in Democracy," it cannot help but reverberate not only upon the other communions within this nation's "public church" but also upon the citizenry as a whole, who continue to seek the blessings of liberty.

What, finally, do the pastoral letters themselves envision as the shape of the "New American Experiment in Democracy"? This theme, at first only implicit in the peace pastoral letter's pledge to create "a community of conscience" within both the church and "the wider civil community,"[35] has become increasingly explicit with each draft of the letter on the economy. The "New American Experiment" emerges as the bishops' long-term strategy for implementing the economic rights that Catholic social teaching asserts along with basic civil rights. Fully aware that economic rights, for example, rights to employment, decent working conditions, and wages consistent with the requirements of "human dignity," are currently recognized neither by U.S. public opinion nor by the Constitution's Bill of Rights, the bishops call for an "experiment in economic democracy" parallel to the experiment in political democracy that the founders of this nation launched in order to protect civil and political rights.[36] Initially, then, the bishops see the "New American Experiment" as a process of spiritual and moral conversion aimed at transforming the American ethos, so that these economic rights can become the object of genuine moral consensus and then be implemented in various public policies.

This vague hope becomes more explicit, however, when the bishops return to the "New American Experiment" toward the end of the policy section of the first draft of the letter. Here the rhetoric of experiment is translated into a proposal for creating new forms of social collaboration on a massive scale, with suggestions for institutionalizing non-adversarial relations between labor and management within individual firms and industries, and public cooperation in developing and coordinating economic planning policies at the local and regional, national, and international levels.[37] In the second and third drafts of the pastoral letter on the economy, the experiment in economic democracy is given even greater emphasis. Here it is lifted out of the section of the letter on specific problem areas and policy recommendations, and presented in a chapter of its own: "A New American Experiment: Partnership for the Public Good."[38]

Though the specific proposals are similar in all three drafts, placing them in a separate chapter makes it clear that the experiment is no longer one policy proposal among others, but the key to implementing any of the bishops' recommendations in the long-term future.

Though hardly a grand design for social revolution, the "New American Experiment" does seek to mobilize the "public church" in behalf of some form of economic planning consistent with the principle of subsidiarity. Here, too, there is considerable evolution in the bishops' thinking from the first to the second and third drafts. While the first draft seems to be overly defensive about the idea of economic planning,[39] the second and third drafts invoke the principle of subsidiarity systematically at all three levels of economic "partnership": local and regional, national, and international. In each case, the appeal to subsidiarity leads the bishops to exhort individuals and voluntary associations to seize the initiative, and to defend government intervention only when "small or intermediate groups in society are unable or unwilling to take the steps needed to promote basic justice."[40] While the bishops could have been more explicit about how this same principle is also operative in their advocacy of various experiments in "partnerships between labor and management" and the democratization of corporate governance, they clearly present a vision of the economy in which the "public church," including the Catholic community, acts as a "mediating structure" facilitating cooperation among individuals, groups, and institutions who heretofore have regarded each other as adversaries. The "New American Experiment" thus turns out to be a host of interrelated social experiments, whose coordination through various public and private agencies, it is hoped, will create the synergisms necessary to stimulate the economy in the direction of basic justice. Though it may tend to make the politicization of the U.S. economy more explicit than is usally the case, it is anything but a blueprint for state socialism.

Perhaps these sketchy proposals advocating "partnership for the public good" can better be appreciated by contrast with those of another advocate of economic democracy. Robert Dahl's recent work, *A Preface to Economic Democracy*, defends the "right to democracy within (business) firms" in the context of his own struggle with Tocqueville's prophecy of "administrative despotism."[41] Unlike Tocqueville's neoconservative admirers, who apparently assume that egalitarianism is subversive of liberty, Dahl tries to defend egalitarianism by questioning the actual linkage between it and the atomistic culture of self-gratification that Tocqueville thought would contribute to the ultimate despotism.

The threat of "administrative despotism," in Dahl's view, consists not in egalitarianism as such, but in our failure to follow through on the principle of democratic self-government in all institutional sectors of society, especially the economy. We seem to be creating a culture that, indeed, is subversive of the American experiment in democracy, by allowing our respect for property rights to override what Dahl regards as our "right to democracy within firms." Here is the core of his argument:

> If democracy is justified in governing the state, then it is also justified in governing economic enterprises. What is more, if it cannot be justified in governing economic enterprises, we do not quite see how it can be justified in governing the state. Members of any association for whom the assumptions of the democratic process are valid have a *right* to govern themselves by means of the democratic process. If, as we believe, those assumptions hold among us, not only for the internal government of economic enterprises, then we have a *right* to govern ourselves democratically within our economic enterprises.[42]

Only if we begin to exercise this right will we begin to form patterns of cooperative association pervasive enough to ensure that the Tocquevillean "rough equality of social condition" necessary to sustain the American experiment in democracy will not end up subverting it.

Though Dahl and the bishops appeal to many of the same specific examples to describe the range of experiments needed to implement economic democracy, their ways of moral reasoning diverge to such an extent as to make a significant practical difference. The bishops, in short, do not advocate a "right" to economic democracy as such, but a cluster of economic rights whose implementation prudentially requires a "New American Experiment in Democracy." Their reasoning about how the experiment might fulfill these rights is goal-oriented, or what contemporary moralists refer to as "teleological." It is also consistent with what we would expect, following the logic of moral discourse constructed in chapter four, of public arguments in behalf of a "generalizable interest." Dahl's argument, by contrast, follows the pattern contemporary moralists identify as duty-based, or "deontological."[43] The practical significance of this formal difference in moral reasoning hinges on the following: if economic democracy is advocated as a matter of "right," then it must be implemented no matter what the consequences. Ultimately, its implementation is not a matter of open-ended experiment; for if it is based on a valid "right's" claim, the only morally acceptable result of the experiment would be to continue the "experiment." Though Dahl does try to deal with the question of economic efficiency and other technical imperatives, the logic of his argument is such that these trade-offs[44] could never be sufficient to overturn a valid "right's" claim. Under these logical assumptions, the "experiment" could never fail.

The bishops' "New American Experiment in Democracy," on the other hand, remains a true experiment. The experiment is proposed as in the generalizable interest of society as a whole: it defines a goal and suggests a set of strategies for fulfilling certain human rights allegedly neglected in the current structure of the U.S. economy. This goal is presented as what could be-

come the object of a true consensus "ascertained *without deception*." The perception of the need for such a "new" experiment
thus necessarily rests upon prudential judgments, as do whatever criteria would be used to monitor the experiment's success
or failure. The result is an argument for an open-ended process
of experimentation that, precisely because it is based on a softer
moral claim than the one allowed by Dahl's deontological
reasoning, is both richer in its appeal to both Catholic tradition
and American experience, and capable of greater flexibility in
responding to the economic trade-offs that are sure to surface
once the experiments get underway. The bishops' recommendations thus are deliberately open-ended: they are a word of encouragement prodding the "public church" and society as a
whole in a direction that, it is hoped, will promote basic justice.
Yet the experiment itself is not to be confused with basic justice;
rather, it is recommended as a promising means to that end —
no more and no less.

Seen in light of these formal considerations, the bishops' refusal to be as bold as Dahl in circumscribing property rights represents not a failure of nerve but the triumph of experiential
learning. For, if the experiment in economic democracy is truly
an experiment, we simply do not yet know how property rights
will be affected, if at all, by various attempts to democratize the
economy. Nor do we yet know what, if any, are the technical
limits to worker participation in managerial decision-making
processes or shareholder participation in corporate governance.
The bishops' wise agnosticism on these technical questions
could have been defended by appeal to the principle of subsidiarity; but in any case, in order for the experiment to begin, they
need not resolve these questions. Given their purposes, all the
bishops need do is define the proper goal for across-the-board experimentation and, using the principle of subsidiarity, establish
the burden of proof that any "higher" authorities must discharge
in order to justify their interventions.

An Americanist Catholic, in my view, would have even
deeper reasons for preferring the bishops' version of economic

democracy to Dahl's. Recall that Dahl's proposal is meant to counter the threat of a Tocquevillean "administrative despotism." By focusing on the business firm or corporation as the centerpiece in any strategy for overcoming this threat to democracy, Dahl seems to be assuming that economic relations, for example those that obtain between workers and managers, are more important strategically than other primary relationships, as in the family, the neighborhood or ethnic group, or especially in religious communities. Yet it is clear that Tocqueville, at least, saw the churches and synagogues as the primary bulwark of the American democratic ethos.

To be faithfully Tocquevillean in overcoming America's failure to be consistently democratic in its institutions, the first target for any "New Experiment in Democracy" should be the churches themselves. Only in the context of an ethos in which the "public church" has had a significant impact, does it make sense to proceed to experiment on economic institutions, where the technical imperatives are, if anything, even more formidable than the ecclesiological objections usually raised against democratization of the church. Though Americanist Catholics may welcome Dahl's proposal as well-intended, they may come to regard its arguments as so abstract that they border on the doctrinaire. At that point, they will turn with relief to the bishops' more nuanced position.

If this reading of the differences between these two approaches to economic democracy is on the mark, then, finally, it should be clear why I regard the bishops' call for a "New American Experiment in Democracy" not just as a convenient occasion for raising the issue of democratization in the church, but also as a model of the appropriate way to raise that issue. For this proposal, like the bishops' own, asks merely for experiment. Like the bishops' proposal, the case of the church's experiment in democracy has been argued in ways meant to be faithful to both Catholic tradition and American experience; like the bishops' it uses a resource specific to Catholic social teaching, namely, the principle of subsidiarity, to clarify both the scope of the experiment and its inevitable limits. Neither the bishop's experiment, nor my own, is argued as a matter of natural "right"; instead, both are presented as possible objects of a true consensus within a church that, presumably, is seeking to become an authentically American community of moral discourse. Just as the bishops have argued their case not simply as an agenda exclusive to Catholic religious praxis, but have insisted that their experiment may hold the key to America's capacity to deliver "basic justice" to all its citizens, so I am arguing that the democratization of the church is not just desirable from the perspective of Catholic ecclesiology, but may also hold the key to various efforts in American Christianity today to renew itself as a "public church" and thus continue the work of building "the kingdom on earth." Just as the bishops have broken new ground in recognizing that, with reference to economic justice, the church must practice what it preaches, so I am making a similar point about the experiment in democracy: If the church expects this nation's economic institutions to democratize themselves so that all may share in "basic justice," the church must lead the way by democratizing its own institutions.

Notes

1. *Pastoral Constitution on the Church in the Modern World (Gaudium et Spes)*, par. 4, in Walter M. Abbott, ed., *The Documents of Vatican II* (London: Geoffrey Chapman, 1967), p. 202.

2. Cf. Luke 12:54-6; and Matthew 16:3.

3. *Pastoral Constitution on the Church in the Modern World (Gaudium et Spes)*, par. 3-4, in Abbott, ed., *op. cit*, pp. 201-2.

4. *Ibid.*, par. 9, p. 207.

5. *Ibid.*, par. 26, pp. 215-6.

6. *Ibid.*, par. 44, p. 246.

7. Peter Hebblethwaite, "The Popes and Politics: Shifting Patterns in 'Catholic Social Doctrine,'" in *Daedalus*, Vol. III, No. 1 (Winter 1982), p. 200.

8. Cf. Brad Reynolds, "Vatican transfers Hunthausen roles to local auxiliary," in the *National Catholic Reporter* (September 12, 1986), pp. 1, 6.

9. Cf. Jay Dolan, *The American Catholic Experience: A History from Colonial Times to the Present* (Garden City, New York: Doubleday, 1985), p. 117; cf. James Hennesey, S.J., *American Catholics: A History of the Roman Catholic Community in the United States* (New York: Oxford University Press, 1981), pp. 89-100.

10. Cf. Hennesey, *op. cit.*, p. 95.

11. *Ibid.*

12. Hans Küng, *Truthfulness: the Future of the Church* (London: Sheed and Ward, 1968), pp. 224-37.

13. Cf. Dolan, *op. cit.*, pp. 115-6.

14. *Ibid.*, p. 110.

15. *Ibid.*, p. 107.

16. Küng, *op. cit.*, p. 225.

17. Dolan, *op. cit.*, p. 106.

18. Küng, *op. cit.*, pp. 226-7.

19. Cf. Martin Marty, *The Public Church: Mainline-Evangelical-Catholic* (New York: Crossroad, 1981); Parker Palmer, *The Company of Strangers: Christians and the Renewal of America's Public Life* (New York: Crossroad, 1983); Richard John Neuhaus, *The Naked Public Square: Religion and Democracy in America* (Grand Rapids, Michigan: Eerdmans, 1984); and Robert N. Bellah, Richard Madsen, William M. Sullivan, Ann Swidler, and Steven M. Tipton, *Habits of the Heart: Individualism and Commitment in American Life* (Berkeley, California: University of California Press, 1985).

20. Alexis de Tocqueville, *Democracy in America*, Volume II (New York: Vintage Books/Random House, 1945), pp. 336-7.

21. Peter Steinfels, "Neo-Conservatism in the United States," in Gregory Baum, ed., *Neo-Conservatism: Social and Religious Phenomenon*, in *Concilium: Religion in the Eighties* (New York: Seabury Press, 1981), pp. 39-42.

22. Cf. Peter L. Berger, *Ethics and the New Class* (Washington, D.C.: Ethics and Public Policy Center, 1982).

23. Neuhaus, *op. cit.*, p. 75.

24. *Ibid.*, p. 113.

25. Cf. H. Richard Niebuhr, *The Kingdom of God in America* (New York: Harper and Row, 1959), pp. 164-98.

26. Neuhaus, *op. cit.*, pp. 123f.

27. *Ibid.*, pp. 235f.

28. *Ibid.*, p. 201.

29. Cf. Richard John Neuhaus, "Foreword," in Philip F. Lawler, *How Bishops Decide: An American Catholic Case Study* (Washington, D.C.: Ethics and Public Policy Center, 1986), pp. iii-vi.

30. *Ibid.*, p. iv.

31. Marty, *op. cit.*, p. ix.

32. *Ibid.*, p. 3.

33. *Ibid.*, pp. 132f.

34. *Ibid.*, p. 14.

35. National Conference of Catholic Bishops, *The Challenge of Peace: God's Promise and our Response* (Washington, D.C.: United States Catholic Conference, 1983), par. 274-329.

36. National Conference of Catholic Bishops, *First Draft — Bishops' Pastoral: Catholic Social Teaching and the U.S. Economy*, in *Origins*, Vol. 14, No. 22/23 (November 15, 1984), par. 89.

37. *Ibid.*, par. 241-69.

38. National Conference of Catholic Bishops, *The Second Draft: Catholic Social Teaching and the U.S. Economy*, in *Origins*, Vol. 15, No. 17 (October 10, 1985), par. 283-313; *The Third Draft: Economic Justice for All: Catholic Social Teaching and the U.S. Economy*, in *Origins*, Vol. 16, No. 3 (June 5, 1986), par. 291-321.

39. National Conference of Catholic Bishops, *The First Draft — Bishops' Pastoral*, par. 261-2.

40. National Conference of Catholic Bishops, *The Second Draft*, par. 302; *The Third Draft*, par. 310.

41. Robert A. Dahl, *A Preface to Economic Democracy* (Berkeley, California: University of California Press, 1985), pp. 7-51.

42. *Ibid.*, pp. 134-5.

43. Cf. Peter Baelz, *Ethics and Belief* (New York: A Crossroad Book/The Seabury Press, 1977), pp. 29-34.

44. Cf. Arthur M. Okun, *Equality and Efficiency: The Big Tradeoff* (Washington, D.C.: The Brookings Institution, 1975).

CONCLUSION

E PLURIBUS UNUM: LITURGY AND SUSTAINING THE CHURCH AS A COMMUNITY OF MORAL DISCOURSE

The liturgy teaches us to have grateful hearts: to thank God for the gift of life, the gift of earth and the gift of all people. It turns our hearts from self-seeking to a spirituality that sees the signs of true discipleship in our sharing of goods and working for justice. By uniting us in prayer with all the people of God, with the rich and the poor, with those near and dear and with those in distant lands, liturgy challenges our way of living and refines our values.

— Paragraph 327, "Economic Justice for All: Catholic Social Teaching and the U.S. Economy: The Third Draft"

I wish I could conclude this theological reflection on the church's "New Experiment in Democracy" fully confident that the good beginning made in the bishops' recent pastoral letters will now inspire further initiatives in that direction. But events of the past few months, the handling of the Charles E. Curran case at the Catholic University of America, the unusual restrictions placed upon the episcopal ministry of Archbishop Raymond Hunthausen in Seattle, and the brief controversy over the question of dissent at the parish level involving Governor Mario Cuomo of New York, among a host of other less publicized incidents, make me wonder whether the pastoral letter process will turn out to be the harbinger of a new springtime for American Catholicism, or the waning days of an Indian summer, a last breath of unseasonably warm weather before the big chill sets in once more. At the moment, there's no telling what we're in for.

In either event, what I have attempted here is meant to put us all on notice. If we are due for an early spring, then I hope that my reflections will help show the church where and how to plant that the harvest of the "New Experiment in Democracy" may be plentiful in its season. If, on the other hand, we are about to be hit with another long and difficult winter, then I want us all to know the meaning of what will by then have been scattered before the icy wind. In addressing these reflections to the American Catholic community, I would hope to reach both bishops and ordinary believers: bishops, inasmuch as it is finally their actions in response to the unprecedented initiatives from Rome that will determine the meaning of this moment; ordinary believers, inasmuch as it is their memories and their daily experience of life in this country that will continually inspire and renew our hopes for a Catholic church that one day may become a genuinely American community of moral discourse. Those hopes will not die, even if the present opportune moment is lost.

There is one last point that I wish to convey out of my own experience of the pastoral letter process. It was unexpected, for it revealed to me a dimension to the questions of "civility," moral consensus, and dissent that transcends the theoretical reflections that I have offered here. At the meetings I attended, especially the conference on "Catholic Social Teaching and the U.S. Economy" held at the University of Notre Dame in December 1983, and a similar one responding to the first draft of the pastoral letter, held at the University of Santa Clara in January 1985, I was deeply impressed by the role of the evening public liturgies in sustaining the community of moral discourse that had been struggling to form itself during the conferences' working sessions. Especially moving for me was the giving of the Sign of Peace after the recitation of the Lord's Prayer. For in that liturgical gesture of reconciliation, ideological differences and conflicting prudential judgments seemed to disappear. Or perhaps they didn't disappear, but were somehow transformed, now becoming part of the celebration of a Body of Christ secure enough in its basic integrity to rejoice in differences of perspective rather than to feel threatened by them.

Perhaps the fact that I was so moved only testifies to my spiritual poverty. Were such gestures of reconciliation more common in my life, they probably would not appear so extraordinary. But they did occasion a thought that I would like to leave with you. My experience suggests that the unity of the church emphatically is not ideological; it neither presupposes nor imposes intellectual conformity. What does keep us united are the public acts of breaking bread together and sharing a cup of wine that constitute our fellowship in the Body of Christ. This point will be worth remembering, as through our worshipping together we try to find the resources we need to cope with either the thaw of early springtime or the chill of lingering winter.

For it is our unity as a worshipping community that will redeem the promise of our "selective Catholicisms," that will encourage us to overcome the threat of ideological polarization, that will allow us to make our unique contributions to the shaping of a "New Experiment in Democracy" that will benefit all of our fellow citizens through its impact on the renewal of our American "public church." If this is, as Richard John Neuhaus suggested, "'the Catholic moment' in American religious and cultural history," how well we conduct ourselves in that moment for the most part will be determined by the consistency of our lives with those routine liturgical gestures of reconciliation. It is my hope that we will become more faithful, and therefore more loving, in our response to the differences that separate us, for ultimately the truthfulness required of a Catholic church striving to become an American community of moral discourse cannot be endured on any other basis.

Home delivery
from
Sheed & Ward

Here's your opportunity to have bestsellers delivered right to you. Our free catalog is filled with the newest titles on spirituality, church in the modern world, women in religion, ministry, small group resources, adult education/scripture, medical ethics videos and Sheed & Ward classics.

Please send me a free Sheed & Ward catalog for home delivery.

NAME _____

ADDRESS _____

CITY _____ STATE/ZIP _____

If you have friends who would like to order books at home, we'll send them a catalog to —

NAME _____

ADDRESS _____

CITY _____ STATE/ZIP _____

NAME _____

ADDRESS _____

CITY _____ STATE/ZIP _____